LEARNING COMMUNITIES

CHANGING THE WAY PEOPLE INTERACT TO CREATE A LEARNING ORGANIZATION

BY
DR. J. MIKE HUTCHINGS

authorHOUSE™

1663 LIBERTY DRIVE, SUITE 200
BLOOMINGTON, INDIANA 47403
(800) 839-8640
WWW.AUTHORHOUSE.COM

First published by AuthorHouse 12/09/05

ISBN: 1-4208-9125-1 (sc)

Printed in the United States of America
Bloomington, Indiana

This book is printed on acid-free paper.

TABLE OF CONTENTS

LIST OF TABLES

PREFACE

For centuries, theologians and biblical scholars have pondered the method Jesus used to influence the world. In biblical times, the Jews expected a great ruler to come to power to free them from their Roman oppressors. Instead, Jesus chose twelve ordinary men to become his disciples who would carry on his work after he was gone. This group of men lived and learned together; and after Jesus' departure, they set out to change the world. None of the disciples became political leaders. Instead, they established small communities throughout the known world. These communities broke bread together and shared what they had in common. And the size of their group grew.

This book attempts to answer why small groups are effective in carrying out the missions of organizations. It is the result of three years of doctoral study on the subject of strategic leadership. Prior to taking up these studies, I owned and operated a small business that provided health care services to developmentally disabled adults and children. After fifteen years at the helm, the company grew from fifteen employees to more than 120. But the combination of internal personnel problems and external problems with government regulators gradually took its toll on me. I had to take a break. There had to be a better way to make a living, I thought. So I set out to broaden my horizons on leadership by enrolling in the Doctor of Strategic Leadership program at Regent University. I had held leadership positions before in professional associations and in my church, but I had no idea of the transformation in store for me in the way I perceived leadership.

The best way to explain this transformation is to share a sailing adventure that my wife and I took with another couple a few years ago. Since I can remember, I have wanted to captain a sailboat through the blue Caribbean waters of the British Virgin Islands. Some friends of ours had made the trip the year before and reported having a wonderful time. So I sold my wife and friends on the vision of a trip of a lifetime, sailing through calm turquoise waters and balmy breezes. I even enrolled in a sailing class to improve my seamanship. But in my optimism, I did not consider the possibility of high winds and high seas. The trip did not turn out to be the perfect voyage I had planned. Instead, I found myself barking out orders to an inexperienced crew who did not appreciate the tone of my voice. I took every problem encountered personally. I had promised a dream vacation, and I was going to do everything in my power to make it happen. But, my efforts were to no avail. This trip was not a good experience, and as a result, I do not have any desire ever to sail again. Fortunately, I was at least able to salvage my relationship with my wife and friends.

In hindsight, I would have done several things differently on this sailing trip. I would have spent more time building the capabilities of the crew by making them better sailors. I would not have sold them on the idea of a perfect voyage, but instead would have invited them to join me in an adventure with no guarantees. And when that trip was over, they would not only be better crew members, they would also develop skills toward becoming the captain of their own ship. Similarly, in hindsight, I also would have done several things differently in my business. I would have spent more time building the capabilities of my employees. I would have invited them to participate more fully in the adventure. I would have empowered them to become leaders.

A learning community is a group of people who come together as friends who are committed to taking an adventure toward something greater than themselves. They tell the truth to each other and are eager to learn, knowing that no one has all the answers. Building a learning organization does not promise a perfect voyage, but it will be an adventure. If you take this trip, you will hopefully begin to the see the possibilities of changing the way people think. This book sets a general direction, but it will be up to you to navigate around issues that impact your organization. This trip is not for the faint of heart. It is for those who love an adventure.

ORGANIZATIONAL DESIGNER

Since the days of Moses, leaders have faced the challenge of trying to stay connected with as many people within the organization as possible while directing the organization toward its goals. Moses, after leading the Israelites out of Egypt, found himself overwhelmed with the task of filling the role of judge, making decisions regarding every personal and legal dispute among the thousands of his people. The people were growing frustrated while Moses was wearing himself out. Jethro, Moses' father-in-law, urged him to instruct his people to behave appropriately by delegating responsibility to capable men. He urged Moses to delegate part of his role as judge to other men who would serve as judges over "thousands, hundreds, fifties and tens."[1] Jethro may have been one of the earliest organizational designers because he changed the way the people interacted with their leadership. The organizational designer integrates policies and strategies in way that makes the systems work.

How leaders interact with people in the organization reveals how much the organization values its members. Early on, Moses may have felt that he was the only person capable of settling disputes among the Israelites. He may have thought that because he was the only one called by God, only he had the wisdom to resolve the disputes. But after Jethro's suggestions, Moses delegated the responsibility to other men to serve as judges, sending a clear message that capable men could assume responsibility.

In the same way that an architect needs to have a good working knowledge of structures and mechanical systems, an organizational designer must have a good working knowledge of paradigms and how they influence organizations. A paradigm is a set of rules and regulations, written or unwritten, that does two things. First, it establishes or defines boundaries of authority. Second, it tells everyone how to behave inside the boundaries in order to be successful.[2] Simply stated, a paradigm is a set of rules to a game. The game of tennis provides a good metaphor. Tennis has a specific set of boundaries, identified by white lines and a set of directions about how to act within those boundaries. Five time Wimbledon champion Bjorn Borg was once asked to share the secret to playing tennis. His answer was simple, "All you have to do is keep the ball within the white lines."[3]

The organizational designer defines appropriate interaction within the boundaries of authority, as well as the appropriate interaction of people with each other. For example, Jesus' new teaching changed the existing paradigm regarding interaction with God and interaction between people. The first century Jew may not have regarded God on a personal level, but Jesus called him Abba, or father, redefining the existing interaction with God. Jesus also redefined the appropriate interaction between people by talking to the Samaritan woman, someone with whom Jews were not allowed to associate.[4]

As an owner and founder of a small business that provides health care services to developmentally disabled adults and children, the boundaries of authority rest with me. I am the ultimate steward of the organization's vision. As such, I decide in what direction the company should go and when the necessary changes should take place. In the past, people were employed to carry out the duties and responsibilities I thought were necessary to fulfill the company's mission. Employee behavior was rewarded when it was compliant, dependable, and loyal. I often directed their activities by telling or selling them on the ideas I considered to be important. This paradigm worked well during the early years of the company, but as the company grew and competition increased, I found myself engulfed in operating problems while losing sight of opportunities in the marketplace. This type of interaction also did little to facilitate employee commitment evidenced by significant staff turnover.

Henry Mintzberg, professor of management studies at McGill University in Montreal, Canada warns that if every need for change rests with the leader, then the advantage of being able to respond quickly becomes a liability. Mintzberg continues:

> This type of organization reached its heyday in the era of the great American trusts of the late nineteenth century, when powerful entrepreneurs personally controlled huge empires. Since then, at least in Western society, the entrepreneurial organization has been on the decline. Nonetheless, it remains a prevalent and important configuration, and will continue to be so as long as society faces the conditions that require it: the prizing of entrepreneurial initiative and the resultant encouragement of new organizations, the need for small and informal organizations in some spheres and of strong personalized leadership.[5]

The entrepreneurial organization had worked well early on for my health care company, but as the dynamics of the company became more complicated and competition became more intense, it became more obvious that it was time to explore another paradigm—a new set of rules for doing business.

Every organization develops different processes to accomplish its objectives. A process is a sequence of events that lead to an achieved outcome. Processes may include strategic planning, conflict resolution, team building, leadership training, and performance management. The way in which members of the organization interact with authority and with each other differentiates organizations from one another as they perform these different processes. In military terms, these processes are known as the *rules of engagement*. In organizational terms, they are known as the *rules of interaction*. All these processes are aligned to form an organization that is continually expanding its capacity to create its future.[6]

The premise of this book is based on two basic assumptions. First, it assumes that wisdom and learning are not the exclusive property of one individual but are the property of every person within the organization. James Surowiecki, in his book *The Wisdom of Crowds*, states, "If you put together a big enough and diverse enough group of people and ask them to make decisions affecting matters of general interest, that group's decisions will, over time, be intellectually superior to the isolated individual, no matter how smart or well-informed the individual."[7]

Second, it assumes that learning organizations are not created by individuals but by learning communities. Peter Senge, author of the best-selling book *The Fifth Discipline*, identified what it takes to create such an organization when he wrote "the real generative point in moving toward a learning organization is in small groups that form around commitments. These are groups of people who are really committed to something larger than themselves and larger than their own personal desires. They support each other in the way that real friends support each other. They tell the truth to each other and they are continually in a mode of enquiry, knowing that nobody knows and everybody can learn continually."[8]

The design of a learning community provides the catalyst to create such an organization. The process of creating this learning organization begins with the creation of a core learning community with each person subsequently creating additional learning communities until the entire organization becomes a network of learning communities. The initial learning community forms the nucleus of the organization. Each member must embrace the values, skills and vision of a learning community before they can begin the process of creating new ones. For example, in the New Testament Jesus called twelve disciples to join him in a learning relationship that eventually changed the world. When Jesus formed this learning community, the goal was not for them to remain a closely knit group but to go into the world to spread the good news. Similarly, a learning community will be commissioned to go into an organization to pass on the good news that there is a new way of interacting.

Many organizations have used small study groups to begin the process of implementing change initiatives in their organizations. Kimbal Fisher, a leading authority on managing self-directed work teams, began the successful implementation of these teams with the formation of a study group. Over a period of six months, these teams met once or twice each month to discuss the twelve books they had jointly decided were essential. During these discussions, they would note specific concepts or models that were directly applicable to their operation. These observations then became the foundation for the vision, the operating principles and strategies.[9]

Similar to self-directed work teams, John Kotter, former professor of leadership at Harvard Business School, suggests establishing a guiding coalition to spearhead a change initiative. Effective guiding coalitions have four characteristics. First, coalitions must include key players who possess enough positional power so that those left out cannot easily block progress. Second, a coalition must have a sufficient number of people with various expertise and work experience that will help in making informed, intelligent decisions. Third, the group must have enough people with good reputations within the firm to ensure credibility. Finally, the coalition must include enough proven leaders to be able to drive the change process.[10]

Werner Heisenberg and a small group of physicists, including Albert Einstein, Wolfgang Pauli and Niels Bohr, conducted a lifetime of conversations together that ultimately uprooted and reshaped traditional physics in the first half of the last century. They realized that people can become more insightful and more intelligent collectively than is possible individually. The interaction between these world-renowned scientists as colleagues contributed to a greater understanding of the field of physics and demonstrated that the collective intelligence of a team can potentially be much greater than the intelligence of the individuals.[11]

Senge proposes that in order to become a learning organization, people must put aside their old ways of thinking (mental models), learn to be open with others (personal mastery), understand how their company really works (systems thinking), form a plan everyone can agree on (shared vision), and then work together to achieve that vision (team learning). Mental models are often formed after years of working in organizational cultures that clearly delineates the roles of management and direct reports. Fisher, in his efforts to transform groups into self-directed work teams, found the transition most difficult for managers who were afraid of losing their power and authority. Managers often have a difficult time giving up the power and authority they worked so hard to achieve, insisting instead that front-line people are required to do what they are told and not to question their supervisor's directives. According to Senge, these mental models are internal views of the world, a view that closely follows psychologist Carl Jung's principle of the archetype. Jung, who developed the concept of the collective unconscious, centered his theories about what drives human behavior on the existence of certain archetypes. He defined an archetype as an inherited way of thinking, a mythic image that exists for all members of a culture.

Peter Block, the author of *The Answer to How is Yes,* also uses Jung's concept of the archetype to identify four ways of thinking. Block explores the following four images of the world: the engineer, the economist, the artist and the architect. Each image represents a strategic stance, a way of thinking, and a way of acting. The engineer is the prototype of the pragmatic life. The heart and soul of an engineering strategy is to control, predict, automate, and measure the world. The engineer wants to know how things work. Change management is about clear goals, consistent practices, predictable results and accurate measurements. The economist, an ally of the engineer, justifies his or her way of thinking on the basis of cost, safety, control and predictability. The economist believes that money, tangible rewards, or other incentives are what motivate people to act. The economist bets on the creative and entrepreneurial contribution of a small group who can lead and direct the majority. The artist, on the other hand, focuses on matters of the heart. Artist here is used in a broad sense to include people who spend their days in the world of feelings, intuition, and the softer disciplines. This archetype includes social scientists, philosophers, therapists, social workers, educators, and spiritual advisors. The painter and the social scientist count on their ability to observe and capture an observation in images or words.

The engineer-economist and the artist are at opposite ends of the spectrum.[12] It is the architect, or the organizational designer, that integrates both worlds. The architect does not have the luxury the engineer has to focus exclusively on the practical properties and how to make them work. Neither does the designer have the luxury the artist has to focus exclusively on the form and subjective aspects of the world. But the organizational designer of a learning community brings aesthetics and utility into harmony with one another. The interactive design of the learning community provides a safe place where people can examine their thinking through open and honest dialogue. Change begins with new thinking directed toward old problems.

ENDNOTES

1   Exod. 18:21 NIV (New International Version).
2   Joel Arthur Barker, *Paradigms: The Business of Discovering the Future* (New York: HarperCollins, 1992), 32.
3   Bjorn Borg, speech given at the Bollettieri Tennis Academy in Braden, Florida, [ca 1992], and heard by author.
4   Mark 14:36; John 4:9 NIV.
5   Henry Mintzberg, *Mintzberg on Management: Inside Our Strange World of Organizations* (New York: The Free Press, 1989), 129.
6   Peter M. Senge, *The Fifth Discipline: The Art and Practice of the Learning Organization* (New York: Doubleday, 1990), 14.
7   James Surowiecki, *The Wisdom of Crowds: Why the Many are Smarter than the Few and How Collective Wisdom Shapes Business, Economics, Societies and Nations* (New York: Doubleday, 2004), xvii.
8   Peter Senge, "The Learning Organization Made Plain," interview by Patricia A. Galagan, *Training & Development* 45, no. 37 (October 1991): 8.
9   Kimball Fisher, *Leading Self-Directed Work Teams:A Guide to Developing New Team Leadership Skills* (New York: McGraw-Hill, 1993), 61.
10 John P. Kotter, *Leading Change* (Boston: Harvard Business School Press, 1996), 57.
11 Senge, *The Fifth Discipline,* 238.
11 Peter Block, *The Answer to How is Yes: Acting on What Matters* (San Francisco: Berrett-Koehler Publishers, 2002), 165.
12 Jeanne Gibbs, "About Tribes" (2005), [article online]; available from http://www.tribes.com/ article_research.htm; Internet.

CHAPTER ONE

Learning Communities

The concept of a learning community is probably more commonly recognized in the field of education than in the field of business. The concept, however, does represent a paradigm shift in the way people in positions of authority interact with subordinates, a shift from the traditional hierarchy of command and control to a more democratic style of interacting.

In the field of education, the traditional paradigm emphasizes teaching by holding the teacher as the information giver and learner as the individual receiver. The new paradigm emphasizes learning by seeing the teacher as co-learner and facilitator and the learning process as a social activity where collaboration enhances the experience. Jeanne Gibbs, in her book *Tribe: A Process for Social Development and Cooperative Learning,* explains how she brought the concept of a learning community to the elementary school classroom with remarkable results. Gibbs introduced training courses that emphasized transferring responsibility from teacher to student groups that would support each others' learning, problem-solve issues, and manage their work together. Some of the outcomes included the following: (a) an average of 75 percent decrease in student behavior problems within three months, (b) an increase in teacher collegiality and parent involvement, (c) an improvement in teacher-student relationships, and (d) an increase in student motivation and appreciation for academic learning. Today thousands of schools in the United States and Canada have become Tribes Learning Communities.[1] These schools have implemented Tribes in response to a paradigm shift away from the traditional thought that uses a control-the-kids-teacher-talk approach to a new interactive approach that connects students with each other and with their teachers. The program allows for collaboration between students which encourages cooperation, discussion, and problem solving. Tribes consists simply of small learning groups that use a democratic group process to promote a safe and supportive environment for growth and learning. Instead of trying to fix kids, the program fixes the environment and the systems that had contributed their problems.[2]

In a similar fashion, Donald R. Nelson and Dennis P. Witmer, professors of business ethics at the University of Denver, implemented a fundamental change in their delivery by moving away from a traditional lecture-based approach to an interactive approach involving a discussion-based learning community. Traditional interaction in education settings is generally instructor-focused that relies on lecture as the backbone of the educational philosophy. The student takes the role of a passive receiver of the wisdom while the instructor maintains a high degree of control over the course content and environment. However, Nelson and Witmer realized that the learning community approach facilitated the active involvement of the student in the learning process by de-emphasizing the instructor to emphasize student-centered learning. The student-centered learning community contained a number of essential components. First, there was a recognition that while professors have significant knowledge and experience, students can become knowledgeable experts who also have valuable insight and understanding. Second, the active and direct participatory decision-making by students shaped the direction of the daily classroom discussion. This learning community approach further increased student responsibility for the substantive content of the course. The desired outcome was a classroom reformulated as a cooperative endeavor with the instructor and student as active co-contributors.[3]

After conducting a review of the literature, Nancy Shapiro and Jodi Levine, co-authors of *Creating Learning Communities*, concluded that the following characteristics make up an effective learning community within an educational setting:

1. Organization of students and faculty into smaller, more personal groups rather than large impersonal ones
2. Encouragement of curriculum integration

3. Establishment of academic and social support networks for students rather than students being left to fend for themselves
4. Creation of an environment for students to learn about college expectations
5. Union with faculty in more meaningful ways rather than little or no relational contact between faculty and students
6. Faculty and student focused on learning outcomes, not just the knowledge acquisition
7. Establishment of an environment for community-based delivery of academic support programs rather than each student being isolated
8. Opportunity for examining the first-year experience[4]

Learning Organization

This student-centered approach implemented by the Tribes program and by Nelson and Witmer should and can be adapted to any organizational setting. Imagine an organization where the manager would abandon the traditional telling or selling approach to adopt a discussion-based learning community. The manager would no longer be the center of focus while the rest of the group remains passive receivers of wisdom. Instead, a management team would become actively involved in the learning process with each member recognized as having valuable insights and understanding. Responsibility would shift away from the manager to the entire team, making the manager and the team co-contributors to the final outcomes of organizational activity. In this same organization, managers and employees would build meaningful relationships and support each other in mutual learning experiences where training was focused on learning outcomes, not just the acquisition of knowledge.

In 1990, Peter Senge's book *The Fifth Discipline* popularized the concept of the learning organization. Since its publication, more than a million copies have been sold, and in 1997 the *Harvard Business Review* identified it as one of the seminal management books of the past seventy-five years.[5] Senge was once asked if the passion for creating a learning organization started with the individual. He responded by saying:

I've come to think of it just slightly differently than that. I think it starts with small groups of people. It's true that there is no substitute for individual caring and commitment, but I have come to think that the real generative point in moving toward a learning organization is in small groups that form around commitments. These are groups of people who are really committed to something larger than themselves and larger than their own personal desires. They support each other in the way that real friends support each other. They tell the truth to each other and they are continually in a mode of enquiry, knowing that nobody knows and everybody can learn continually.[6]

Senge's description of a learning community includes the concepts that define the rules of interaction. Those rules include: (a) forming a small group around commitments instead of a large group formed around compliance; (b) committing to something larger than itself and larger than personal desires; (c) supporting each other in the way that real friends support each other rather than treating others as adversaries; (d) telling the truth to each other rather than telling white lies with hidden agendas; (e) being continually in a mode of enquiry, knowing that nobody knows all the answers and everybody can always learn; and (f) being unwilling to claim to be experts who think they know it all and who have actually stopped learning.

The glue that holds this group together is commitment. Rosabeth Kanter, professor of sociology and organization and management at Yale University describes commitment as "the connection between self-interest and group interest. . . . When a person is committed, what he wants to do (through internal feeling) is the same as what he has to do (according to external demands), and thus he gives to the group what it needs to maintain itself at the same time that what he needs to nourish his own sense of self."[7]

There are different degrees of commitment: instrumental, affective and moral. Instrumental commitment occurs when the profits and costs are considered and participants find the cost of leaving the system to be greater than the cost of remaining. Affective commitment primarily centers on a person's relationships, group solidarity and ties of emotion that bind members to each other and to the community they form. Moral commitment upholds the norms, obeys the authority of the group, and supports its values. Total commitment occurs when groups have all three kinds of commitment. Kanter summarizes by stating, "If the group is such that a person feels he can make an instrumental commitment, he becomes invested in it and finds his membership rewarding. If the group is such that he can make an affective commitment, he gains strong social ties, relatedness, and a sense of belonging. If the group is such that he can make a moral commitment, he gains purpose, direction, and meaning, a sense that his acts stem from essential values. To some extent, a person's identity is composed of his commitments."[8]

The concept of the learning community attempts to obtain total commitment from its members. Instrumental commitment can be accomplish if the benefits of being a part of the community outweigh the costs of membership such as financial compensation, good work environment, and training and learning opportunities. Affective commitment should be the result of building meaningful relationships and working with people who support each other like friends. Moral commitment may be the most difficult level to obtain but members can begin by looking beyond their own self interests to see the greater goal of the organization. The learning community is committed to something larger than itself and larger than personal desires. After reflecting on the challenges facing a company like General Electric, CEO Jack Welch stated that the first step, before all other steps, is for the company to "define its destiny in broad but clear terms. You need an overarching message, something big, but simple and understandable."[9]

Jim Collins and Jerry Porras, in their best-selling book *Built to Last*, call these larger than life desires "Big Hairy Audacious Goals" (BHAG). Highly visionary companies often use bold missions as a particularly powerful mechanism to stimulate progress. All companies have goals, but there is a difference between merely having a goal and becoming committed to a huge, daunting challenge. A true BHAG is clear and compelling and serves as the unifying focal point of effort which often creates immense team spirit. It has a clear finish line so the organization can know when it is has achieved the goal. A BHAG engages people—it reaches out and grabs them in the gut. It is tangible, energizing, and highly focused. People "get it" right away because it takes little or no explanation.

It is not just the presence of a goal that stimulates progress; it is also the level of commitment to the goal. Indeed, a goal cannot be classified as a BHAG without a high level of commitment. A BHAG should fall well outside the comfort zone. It should be so bold and exciting that it would continue to stimulate progress even if the organization's leaders disappeared before it had been completed. As such, a BHAG should be consistent with a company's core ideology.[10]

In a learning community, members are committed to the task of something greater than themselves. This process begins by matching each member's personal vision to the vision of the organization. In a business organization, this may require setting extraordinary corporate goals like BHAGs. In religious organizations it may mean serving the mission of the church. Energy is generated by moving beyond oneself, finding greater meaning and purpose in something bigger and making a significant contribution to that cause. For members of the learning community, doing this provides an opportunity to define their destiny— a simple overarching message, something meaningful, but simple and understandable.

As mentioned above, members in the learning community support each other in the way that real friends support each other. Supporting each other like friends means more than cooperating and collaborating together. It requires being authentic and treating people like friends. Carolyn Shaffer and Kristin Anundsen, in their book *Creating Community Anywhere,* define community as "a dynamic whole that emerges when a group of people share common practices, are interdependent, make decisions jointly, identify themselves with something larger than the sum of their individual relationships, and make a long-term commitment to well-being (their own, one another's, and the group's)." In the past, involvement in community was determined by where a person lived or by family or religious connections. Today, however, communities are formed around issues of identity and shared values; they are not location-based. Thus, involvement in communities today takes a conscious commitment to a group. Shaffer and Anundsen refer to this as a conscious "community-meaning" community that emphasizes members' need for personal growth and transformation, the social and survival aspects of community. Today, societal and scientific advances are having a significant impact on the way people interact and the ways they define community.[11]

The learning community's ability to support each other the way friends do facilitates cooperation as well as contributes to a more pleasurable working environment which can help avoid potential conflicts. Members of the learning community tell the truth to each other instead of telling little white lies. Telling the truth requires having the ability to honestly assess the difference between the ideal and current reality. It is important that members do not get caught up in their previous successes in a way that disallows them to see a realistic picture of their organization and its problems.

The members of the learning community are also continually in a mode of inquiry, knowing that nobody knows all the answers and everybody can always learn. This involves a natural state of wanting to know how things and people function. It means wanting to know all you can on a personal level, interpersonal level, and an organizational level. This also involves the humility that comes with knowing that no one person has all the answers and that everyone can learn. Today, learning has become synonymous with the acquisition of knowledge, but the deeper meaning of learning involves a fundamental shift of mind.

Learning Communities vs. Other Groups

Learning communities are different from other types of groups that meet to accomplish specific tasks. Etienne Wenger, in her book *Communities of Practice: Learning, Meaning and Identity*, identifies communities of practice as "groups of people who share a concern, a set of problems, or a passion about a topic, and who deepen their knowledge and expertise by interacting on an ongoing basis." [12] Communities of practice are primarily focused on the task of solving a set of problems. They think of the community in terms of a social configuration and not a function of interrelationships. But a learning community considers building authentic relationships as an important component to establish before trying to accomplish a task. Learning takes place in the context of community. It is within the safe confines of a supportive environment where people are allowed the freedom to experience a "mind shift" without feeling personally threatened.

Hot groups are another highly task-oriented group with a special state of mind: task-obsessed and full of passion. They are always coupled with a distinctive way of behaving; a style that is intense, sharply focused and full-bore. The two major characteristics of hot groups are total preoccupation with the task and a sense of ennoblement. They believe the task to be immensely significant, demanding their complete and undivided attention. Hot groups are preoccupied with their tasks which are accompanied by extremely high performance standards. Their ennoblement comes from a higher sense of purpose. The journey is supremely worthwhile as if on a mission from God. But the interaction that takes place in a hot group is not touchy feely. Rather, hot group members love their task but they don't necessarily love one another. The members are likely to be internally confrontational, challenging, and critical, all with the aim of improving their work. Hot groups do not usually pay much attention to their own or other people's feelings.

In contrast, learning communities usually build trusting interpersonal relationships first and only later concern themselves with their group's task. Hot groups do this in reverse. They first unite around the task, and then work back to their interpersonal relationships. Their hearts, not their egos, are in the work. Hot groups hardly ever suffer from groupthink. Groupthink, as Irving Janis in his book *Groupthink* described it, is the propensity of a group to reach consensus and make decisions too superficially and too quickly.[13] Learning communities guard against groupthink by creating a safe environment where people are not afraid to express different points of view. Learning communities share the same passion for the task but not at the expense of interpersonal relationship. Hot groups typically do not last long. They work at a red hot pace, and then when the project is complete, they disband. But a learning community will stay together and continue to learn by building on past knowledge in order to meet new challenges.

Making the Journey to a Learning Organization

The selection process is important to the success of the learning community. The manner in which people are invited to participate in a learning community is different than the typical request from an employer. Typically, the boss makes a statement like, "I would *really* like you to participate in this project." The underlying message is that if the employee does not participate, he or she might need to find another job with another company. Making participation mandatory may cause resentment and destroy any chance of achieving commitment on the part of the participants. However, if a learning community is to be the catalyst for transforming the organization into a learning organization, then every key person should be included. Some people may be resistant to the process for a variety of legitimate reasons, such as time availability, interest, personality or perceived loss of power. But if commitment is crucial to the success of the learning community, then it becomes necessary to obtain an instrumental level of commitment from those key people before the community is formed. Each person is not required to be totally sold on the idea. But if they can commit to taking the journey to explore the possibilities, then the group can move forward. Concerns and questions can be dealt with along the way as the group learns to dialogue together. If significant opposition exists to this journey, it may be wise to forego the trip.

The last consideration is the commitment of the chief executive officer to the learning community. This person is the cornerstone of the learning community and without his or her full commitment and participation, the group will not have the power or authority to make the kind of changes that arise from the learning community. No captain, no trip.

Once the members of the learning community have been selected the journey begins. The following chapter discusses the process of building a learning community. It begins with building relationships in a safe environment where people can learn more about themselves and others within the community.

ENDNOTES

1 Jeanne Gibbs, *Tribes: A New Way of Learning and Being Together* (Windsor: CenterSource Systems, 2001), 19.

2 Donald R. Nelson and Dennis P Witmer, "Developing a Learning Community Approach to Business Education" *Teaching Business Ethics* 5 (August 2001): 3.

3 Jodi H Levine and Nancy Shapiro, *Creating Learning Communities: A Practical Guide to Winning Support, Organizing for Change, and Implementing Programs* (San Francisco: John Willey & Sons, 1999), 23.

4 Mark K. Smith, "Peter Senge and The Learning Organization" (2005) [article online]; available from http://infed.org/thinkers/senge.htm; Internet.

5 Peter Senge, "The Learning Organization made Plain," interview by Patricia A. Galagan, *Training & Development* 45, no. 37 (October 1991): 37-38.

6 Rosabeth Moss Kanter, *Commitment and Community: Communities and Utopias in Sociological Perspective* (Cambridge: Harvard University Press, 1972), 66.

7 Rosabeth Moss Kanter, *Commitment and Community* (Cambridge: Harvard University Press, 1972), 69-70,

8 James C. Collins and Jerry I. Porras, *Built to Last: Successful Habits of Visionary Companies* (New York: HarperCollins, 1997), 95.

9 Ibid, 91-114.

10 Carolyn Shaffer and Kristin Anundsen, *Creating Community Anywhere : Finding Support and Connection in a Fragmented World* (Berkley: Penquin Group, 1993), 112.

11 Etienne Wenger, *Communities of Practice: Learning, Meaning, and Identity* (New York: Cambridge University Press, 1998), 6-7.

12 Irvin Janis, *Groupthink*, 2nd ed. (Boston: Houghton Mifflin, 1982); quoted in Jean Lipman-Blumen and Harold J. Leavitt, *Hot Groups: Seeding Them, Feeding Them, & Using Them to Ignite Your Organization* (New York: Oxford University Press, 1996), 9-36.

13 Peter M. Senge "Mental Models" *Planning Review* 20, no. 2 (March/April 1992): 4, 8.

CHAPTER TWO

Building a Learning Community

The process of building a learning community begins with an awareness of the basic rules of interaction. In order to create a safe environment where people are treated with dignity and respect, it is first necessary to establish some ground rules of interaction.

Rule 1. Members of the group are to help each other learn. This is not an individual competitive process but one in which collaborative learning is desirable.

Rule 2. Members can openly discuss mistakes without reprimand or ridicule. People need not be afraid to admit mistakes openly and honestly without someone criticizing or ridiculing them.

Rule 3. Members view problems as opportunities to learn. It is important to be future-oriented, not too focused on the past.

Rule 4. Members give open and honest feedback to each other. Feedback is given in the way friends would give feedback, not as an opportunity to punish or ridicule.

Rule 5. Members are encouraged to ask why regardless of their position in the organization. People are encouraged to ask questions to members who are in positions of authority without feeling intimidated or fearful of possible reprimand.

Rule 6. Whenever members state their view, they must also ask what others think. Members actively solicit honest feedback because they truly want to know what others think of their views. This begins the process of learning how to think together rather than just thinking alike.

Rule 7. Members must treat each other with respect. There is no room for disrespect. The community will learn to support each other as friends would.

Rule 8. Members will spend time building trust with each other. This may include experiential exercises or candid conversations about trusting one another.

Rule 9. Members are given time to support learning. Time must be set aside for reflection and learning opportunities.

Rule 10. Members must listen to the views of others before speaking. People in the group must agree to listen fully to what others have to say before they formulate a response.

Community and Communicating

Once the ground rules are established, it may also be helpful to develop a written agreement or to post the rules in plain sight for easy reference. Individuals who break the rules need to be held accountable by the rest of the group. Members do not need to be punished, but sufficient attention should be drawn to any violations. For example, McNair Wilson, formerly an *imagineer* for the Disney Corporation, instituted a one-dollar fine on anyone who blocked the ideas of any person while participating in creative brainstorming sessions. This inexpensive consequence proved to be an effective way to level the playing field, even when CEO Michael Eisner participated. The written agreement would require a commitment from members to attend all learning community sessions. Without a commitment from each member, including the chief executive officer, the learning community has little chance of succeeding.

The word *community* and *communication* come from the same Latin root word *communis,* which means common. In essence, communities are formed by people who communicate with each other. Consequently, people who do not communicate with each other are not part of a community, even if they live next door. Today, communities are no longer bound by geography. People who communicate world-wide electronically can now form virtual communities.

Part of the process of building effective communication into the learning community includes helping the group understand the dynamics of the interaction. Balancing inquiry and advocacy helps facilitate effective communication. Most managers are trained to be advocates. They often debate forcefully and influence others while inquiry skills go unrecognized and unrewarded. But as issues become more complex, managers find they need to tap into the insights of others. Advocacy skills suddenly become counterproductive. Managers can actually close off learning from one another.

In short, flexibility is needed to balance advocacy with inquiry. When two advocates meet for an open exchange, little learning takes place. As each person advocates his or her viewpoint more strongly, positions become more rigid. The practice can leave people without a sense of partnership. Anyone who has ever listened to staunch political opponents discuss controversial issues has witnessed a great deal of advocacy and very little inquiry. Advocacy without inquiry begets more advocating. As the escalations become grueling, people become less willing to state differences and more willing to avoid an ensuing conflict. To stop escalating debates, people must begin asking the question, What is it that leads you to that position? In other words, can the person provide some data or experience in support of his or her position? The most productive learning usually occurs when managers combine their advocacy *and* inquiry skills. Only then can people make their thinking explicit and subject to public examination. When genuine inquiry and advocacy are present, creative outcomes are much more likely.[1]

Balancing dialogue and discussion is also helpful in creating effective communication in the community. The word *discussion* has the same root as percussion and concussion. The purpose is normally to have a person's view prevail over someone else's view. The word *dialogue* comes from the Greek word *dialogos*. *Dia* means *through* and *logos* means *word* and is the noun form of the verb *lego* which simply means *to speak*. Peter Senge states, "Dialogue is the capacity of members to suspend assumptions and enter into genuine 'thinking together.' To the dialogue, different views are presented as a means toward discovering a new view."[2]

Reuel Howe, in his book *The Miracle of Dialogue*, states that the purpose of dialogue "is to restore the tension between vitality and form, to bring parties of a relationship into communicative relation with one another, to shake them free of their conformity and make them available for transformation. Only through dialogue can the miracle of renewal be accomplished in a relationship."[3] Establishing this level of communication is necessary as the group begins to move through the stages of building community.

Stages of Community-Building

M. Scott Peck, in his book *The Different Drum*, explains that the model for community-making includes four distinct stages: (a) pseudo-community, (b) chaos, (c) emptiness, and (d) community.[4]

Psuedo-community. In pseudo-community, members attempt to become an instant community by being extremely pleasant with one another and avoiding all disagreement. This is an unconscious, gentle process that occurs when people who want to lovingly attempt to become a community do so by telling little white lies and by withholding some truth about themselves and their feelings in order to avoid conflict. The essential dynamic of a pseudo-community is conflict avoidance. Genuine communities may experience periods that are free from conflict, but this is because they have learned how to deal with conflict, rather than avoid it. Pseudo-community avoids conflict; true community resolves them. Symptoms of the pseudo-community include the minimization and the lack of acknowledgement, or the ignoring of individual differences. The basic rule is not to do or say anything that might offend someone else. It is easy to see how this approach makes for a smooth functioning group. But it also crushes individuality, intimacy, and honesty. The pretense of a pseudo-community is the denial of individual differences. People tend to speak in generalities using *we* messages instead of *I* messages. To avoid the risk of conflict, members keep their feelings to themselves and even nod in pretense agreement.

Chaos. In truth, though, the use of *I* and *my* statements encourages individual differences to surface in such away that the group almost immediately moves to the second stage of community development: chaos.[5] Chaos always centers on well-intentioned but misguided attempts to heal and convert. By and large, people resist change. But chaos is not just a state; it is an essential part of the process of community development. Unlike those in pseudo-community, in this stage individual differences are out in the open. Only instead of trying to hide or ignore them, the group attempts to obliterate them. The motive is to make everyone normal, which also includes the motive to win as the members fight over whose norm will prevail. The chaos stage is a time of fighting and struggle. The struggle is noisy, uncreative and unconstructive. In a genuine community, disagreement is loving, respectful and quiet as members work hard to listen to each other. Since chaos is unpleasant, it is common for members of a group in this stage to attack each other and their leader. While chaos could be easily circumvented by an authoritarian leader—a dictator who may assign them specific tasks and goals— a dictatorship is not, and never can be, a community. Community and totalitarianism are incompatible. Fighting is far better than pretending the group is not divided.[6]

Emptiness. The next phase, emptiness, can be either the barrier or the gateway to community, depending on how fear is handled. Emptiness requires emptying oneself of the barriers to communication like feelings, assumptions, ideas and motives. If fear of the unknown, fear of failure, and fear of conflict can be acknowledged and engaged with curiosity and reflection, a sense of openness will be fostered. This openness can lead to genuine listening and can increase the capacity to generate shared meaning within the community. If fear is met with a need to control, fix, pretend, lie, or avoid, then the tendency to generate answers rather than questions or to advocate rather than inquire will typically win. Emptiness, the removing of these barriers to communication, is a healthy sign of development. Typically, people panic when they sense it. Too often, a traditional facilitator will lead the retreat back to pseudo-community, pretending things are better than they are. Or, this person will return to chaos, choosing to convert members to a "right" point of view because it is too difficult to be in the place of not knowing. Open dialogue, however, can offer a bridge from chaos through emptiness and ultimately to community. When groups learn to dialogue together, learning occurs because individuals have emptied themselves of their assumptions, feelings and motives long enough to create room for perceiving and acting anew.[7]

Community. The transformation of a group from a collection of individuals into genuine community requires humility, or little deaths, from many of its members. But the transformation is also a process of group death. What this means is that given the right circumstances and knowledge of the rules, on a certain level human beings are able to die for each other. In other words, we are capable of setting aside our own self-interests for the good of the whole. When this death has been completed, when members are open and empty, the group enters community.[8]

Determining the Values, Behavior and Mental Models of the Community

Once the group enters community, it has built a sufficient foundation to begin examining individual differences such as values, behavioral styles, and mental models. Values are the beliefs and standards that guide individual lives and organizations. According to Aubrey Malphurs, author of *Values-Driven Leadership*, values "beget attitudes that specify behavior. They affect everything about the organization: the decisions made, the goals set, the priorities established, the problems solved, the conflicts resolved, and more."[9] Tom Peters, in his best-selling book *In Search of Excellence* states, "Every excellent company we study is clear on what it stands for, and takes the process of values-shaping seriously. In fact, we wonder whether it is possible to be an excellent company without clarity on values and without having the right sort of values."[10]

Milton Rokeach, author of *Understanding Human Values*, has indicated that differences among individuals may not exist so much in the presence or absence of particular values as in the arrangement of them, their hierarchies or priorities. "The ultimate function of human values is to provide us with a set of standards to guide us in all our efforts to satisfy our needs and at the same time maintain and, insofar as possible, enhance self-esteem."[11] The values that identify major end-states of human existence are terminal values, and the behavioral modes for achieving them are instrumental values. Rokeach also developed a values survey, a measuring instrument consisting of eighteen terminal values and eighteen instrumental values. In his studies, he found that the most sensitive indicator of an institution's values was the image of the institution promoted by its gatekeepers, in addition to the personal values of those gatekeepers.

In short, the learning community is the organization's gatekeepers. A similar values audit of the learning community would serve several purposes. First, an audit would create unity by identifying the values held by each member that are in alignment. Second, it would identify those values held in opposition to one another, which may, in turn, represent a source of conflict. The following list represents the hierarchy of the operational values of a learning community. These operational values describe the accepted conduct within the organization. A person who might prioritize conflicting values such as power or competition may see their values in opposition to those of the learning community. Below is a list of the learning community's operational values:

1. Cooperation: working well with others
2. Credibility: being trustworthy and believable
3. Risk-taking: encouraging experimentation and allowing mistakes
4. Knowledge: making effective use of information
5. Accountability: taking responsibility and initiative
6. Compassion: caring about the feelings of others

There are also several different assessment tools available today that measure individual behavioral styles. One such measurement is the DISC Personality System, which identifies four different behavioral styles: dominance, influence, steadiness, and compliance. The underlying theory, developed by Dr. William Marston in his book *The Emotions of Normal People,* views people as behaving along two axes. People's actions tend to be either active or passive, depending upon individual perception of the environment as either antagonistic or favorable. Marston identifies four behavioral factors: dominance, influence, steadiness and compliance. Everyone exhibits all four behavioral factors in varying degrees of intensity. The dominance scale reflects how people respond to problems or challenges. People who score high on this scale are described as adventuresome, competitive, decisive and results-oriented. The influence scale evaluates how people influence others to accept their point of view. People who score high in this area are described as charming, enthusiastic, persuasive, and sociable. The steadiness scale answers how people respond to the pace of the environment. These people are described as patient, stable, sincere, and friendly. The compliance scale reflects how people respond to rules and procedures set by others. People who score high in this area are described as analytical, precise, conscientious and diplomatic. Combinations of two or more of these behavioral styles define personality types that can help members better understand and appreciate themselves and others. Understanding the different dynamics present in the group and learning to adapt to these different styles is important if the group is to succeed.[12]

One thing most managers know is that many of the best ideas never get put into practice and that brilliant strategies often fail to get translated into action. This may be a result of the conflicting influence of people's mental models, deeply held internal images of how the world works—images that limit them to familiar ways of thinking and acting. Mental models shape how people act.[13] Managing mental models requires surfacing, testing and improving internal pictures of how the world operates. Kimball Fisher believes the single reason self-directed work teams often don't work is a lack of management commitment to the whole change process. Impatience or an unwillingness to make the personal management changes necessary to make them work has foiled many attempts to create sustainable self-directed work teams. Team members are forced to make very personal changes. Fisher compared this to moving a cemetery. He says, "You have to move one body at a time. In fact it is harder for management to change to self-directed work teams than for anybody else. Some have abandoned the effort because they were more interested in maintaining management control than in taking the uncomfortable personal risks required to get improved results from empowerment."[14]

Personal mastery requires approaching one's life as a creative work, living life from a creative rather than reactive viewpoint. When personal mastery becomes a discipline—an activity that can be integrated into a person's life—it embodies two underlying movements. The first movement is a continual clarification of what is personally important. The second is continually learning how to see the current reality more clearly. The vision of what is wanted, along with a clear picture of where a person is relative to that want, generates what is called creative tension, a force that can bring the two visions together. The essence of personal mastery is learning how to generate and sustain this creative tension. Learning in this context does not mean acquiring more information, but expanding the ability to produce the results truly wanted in life.[15]

Michael O'Brien recognizes personal mastery as having four adaptive skills: raising consciousness, using imagery, framing and reframing events, and integrating new perspectives. Raising consciousness is catching oneself in the act of thinking and paying attention to emotions. Using imagery is setting aside time each day to dream in detail about what is wanted. Framing and reframing occurs when something important happens to an individual, and when as many internal interpretations as possible are assigned to those events. Integrating new perspectives is learning to incorporate the useful perspectives of others.[16] Because the learning community is in a continuous state of inquiry, members must not only answer questions about the workings of the organization, but must also actively explore the inner workings of their own minds.

The antithesis of a learning community is exclusivity. Learning communities are more likely to arise when certain critical conditions are present within a group, including but not limited to curiosity, commitment, and a desire to act collaboratively with a spirit of experimentation. Learning community members are connected by matters of the heart, as well as the mind. Creating a foundation that can support community is the first step in sustaining learning within the community. Briefly, shared curiosity which motivates collaborative designs can inspire joint experimentation. This, in turn, can lead to the kind of reflection that generates shared insight, which will improve collaborative designs for future experimentation.[17]

ENDNOTES

[1] Peter M Senge, *The Fifth Discipline: The Art and Practice of the Learning Organization* (New York: Doubleday, 1990), 10.

[2] Reuel L Howe, *The Miracle of Dialogue* (New York: The Seabury Press, 1963), 64.

[3] M. Scott Peck, *The Different Drum: Community Making and Peace.* (New York: Simon & Schuster, 1987), 86.

[4] Ibid., 91.

[5] Ibid., 94.

[6] Stephanie Ryan, "Emergence of Learning Communities" *Community Building: Renewing Spirit & Learning in Business,* ed. G. Kaximierz (San Francisco: New Leaders Press, 1995), 85-94.

[7] M. Scott Peck, *The Different Drum*, 103.

[8] Aubrey Maphurs, *Values-Driven Leadership: Discovering and Developing Your Core Values for Ministry* (Grand Rapids: Baker Books, 1996), 20.

[9] Thomas J Peters and Robert Waterman, *In Search of Excellence: Lessons from America's Best-Run Companies* (New York: HarperCollins, 1988), 12.

[10] Milton Rokeach, *Understanding Human Values: Individual and Societal* (New York: Collier Macmillan, 1979), 17.

[11] William Mouton Marston, *The Emotions of Normal People* (Minneapolis: Persona Press, 1979).

[12] Senge, *The Fifth Discipline*, 174.

[13] Kimball Fisher, *Leading Self-Directed Work Teams A Guide to Developing New Team Leadership Skills* (New York: McGraw-Hill, 1993), 46.

[14] Senge, *The Fifth Discipline*, 141.

[15] Michael O'Brien, "Personal Mastery: The New Executive Curriculum" *Training* 33, no. 7 (July 1996): 82.

[16] Stephanie Ryan, "Emergence of Learning Communities," 86.

[17] Kimball Fisher, *Leading Self-Directed Work Teams: A Guide to Developing New Team Leadership Skills* (New York: McGraw-Hill, 1993), 3.

CHAPTER THREE

Going Beyond Teams

During the 1960s, Proctor and Gamble experimented with self-directed work teams. The results of the experiment were so impressive that the company declared them trade secrets with all the same restrictions and security precautions associated with product formulations and marketing plans. Voluntary effort, found within these self-directed work teams, comes from employee commitment, and commitment comes from empowerment. Today it is estimated that virtually every major corporation in North America and Western Europe uses various forms of empowerment somewhere in the organization. Unlike a number of current management experiments, the concept of empowerment is potentially as profound a change in contemporary organizations like Proctor and Gamble as the first industrial revolution was at the turn of the century.[1]

Not all teams perform the way they were intended primarily because they lack empowerment. Learning communities, however, have the potential to go beyond teams because they fully embrace empowering members. Empowerment is a function of four important variables: authority, resources, information, and accountability. Learning communities receive their authority from the top management's commitment to the process of change. Empowerment is based on the assumption that "if you put together a big enough and diverse enough group of people and let them to make decisions affecting matters of general interest, that group's decisions will, over time, be intellectually superior to the isolated individual, no matter how smart or well-informed the individual."[2] Along with the authority necessary to implement changes, the learning community has the full resources of the organization at its disposal to implement those changes. The learning community has direct access to any information it deems necessary to make informed decisions. They draw their conclusion directly from the available data without being screened by top management, although top management remains an integral part of the learning community network. The learning community accepts accountability, knowing they can learn from their mistakes without reprimand or ridicule.

The Problem with Teams

Harvey Robbins and Michael Finley, in their book *Where Teams Go Wrong,* identified several symptoms of the problems relating to where teams go wrong. The following eleven symptoms are indicative of underlying problems that could be solved by improving the variables that enhance empowerment.

Symptom One. Robbins and Finley identified a lack of understanding in teams of what people are supposed to do, or that the tasks given make no sense. Confused goals and cluttered objectives could be solved by clarifying the team's purpose and expected outcomes. This implies, though, that the goals and objectives are handed down from above. In a learning community, members would be full participants in the development of goals and objectives which would automatically eliminate such confusion. When team members are uncertain of what their jobs entail, unresolved roles become a problem. Top management can set broad parameters, but exactly how goals and objectives are accomplished is up to the learning community.

Symptom Two. Another problem occurs when teams make the right decisions but in the wrong way. Bad decision making could be solved by having the team choose an approach appropriate for each decision. In a learning community, establishing a decision-making approach starts with the strategic planning process. Top management gives the learning community as much latitude as possible in order to empower the group. In this group, consensus is the preferred method of making decisions. Although this is time consuming and requires skill and energy, this approach elicits commitment from all members. Making decisions by majority rule may take less time, but what is saved in time is lost in alienating the minority of the learning community. The minority could then jeopardize the group's effectiveness in the future.

Symptom Three. In another symptom, Robbins and Finley identified that uncertain boundaries can result when an empowered team has no clue just how empowered they are. This could be solved by setting quantifiable limits to team power. The learning community, however, is already constantly testing the validity of vertical and horizontal boundaries to determine if they are obstacles to achieving their goals.

Symptom Four. Also, a team that is at the mercy of an employee handbook from hell is the victim of bad policies and stupid procedures. This could be solved by throwing away the book in order to start making sense. But the learning community sees policies and procedures as guidelines. If policies and procedures become obstacles, the community has the ability to revise them quickly so that they assist the group in achieving their goals, as opposed to blocking progress. Because policies and procedures define the corporate culture, the learning community uses them to guide members through this culture. Without these as guides, people may fall back into the previous mental models contrary to the values of this new culture. Policies and procedures are supposed to serve the group, not the other way around.

Symptom Five. The problem of a team not getting along because of personality conflicts could be solved by teaching the team what to expect from one another and by identifying what they prefer and how they differ. Only then can the team start valuing and using the differences. In a learning community, the group spends a great deal of time building the relationships before the learning process begins. The foundation of mutual respect, dialogue and understanding individual differences would have already been established. When a conflict does present itself, the learning community is primarily concerned with maintaining relationships; they are not satisfied with simply keeping the peace. Conflict is resolved by understanding people's values, needs, wants, and perceptions.

Symptom Six. The symptom of tentative or inconsistent leadership reflects poor leadership. This could be solved by teaching the leader to serve the team and to keep their vision alive. If not, that leader can leave leadership to someone else. In a learning community, leadership is shared and the dynamics of the group allow for open and honest feedback about leadership effectiveness. Coaching also provides each member with feedback regarding their leadership skills. Leadership is a learned behavior which is facilitated by practice and accurate feedback within a safe environment. The symptom of leadership selling a bill of goods to the team could be remedied in order to clarify the vision of the organization. But, again, the underlying assumption is that vision is created by top management and sold to the people below. In contrast, the goal of the learning community is a shared vision, not a sold vision. The challenge is to get as many people in the room as possible when creating a shared vision. In a learning community, the personal visions of each member are aligned with that of the organization, resulting in greater clarity and commitment.

Symptom Seven. Robbins and Finley also identified that when an organization is not really committed to the idea of teams, an anti-team culture is created. This problem could be solved either by never forcing people onto a team or by making sure that teams are formed for the right reasons. The underlying assumption of this is that the organization values competition over cooperation and collaboration. The learning community believes in the wisdom of crowds; the more people involved in the process, the higher the quality of the decision.

Symptom Eight. When performance is not measured, team members tend to grope in the dark for lack of sufficient feedback and information. This problem could be solved by creating a system of free flowing information among all team members. The underlying assumption is that people are reluctant to give feedback or to share information for reasons such as fear, competition, conflict, and politeness. But in a learning community, the free flow of information is critical. During the community building process, many obstacles to communication should have been eliminated so people can feel safe in being open and honest with each other.

Symptom Nine. The problem of people being rewarded for the wrong things is the result of an ill conceived reward system. This can be solved by redesigning the reward system to make teams feel safe while doing their job, rewarding team as well as individual behaviors. The underlying assumption here is that top management decides what behaviors get rewarded. In a learning community, the group would decide what behaviors are rewarded. Individual rewards would not necessarily be excluded because the group would decide what individual behavior warrants special compensation. This helps eliminate competition in favor of individual contribution to the group.

Symptom Ten. The symptom of a team not becoming a team results when members are unable to commit, a problem stemming from a lack of team trust. This problem could be solved by curbing untrustworthiness, disbanding or reforming the team. The underlying assumption is that the team was formed without any attempt to establish trust in the beginning. In a learning community, trust is established early on during the community building process.

Symptom Eleven. Finally, when a team knows what to do but lacks the will to it, this is a symptom of unwillingness to change. The problem can be solved by finding out what the blockage is and use dynamite or Vaseline to clear it. In other words, solving this problem can be next to impossible. In a learning community, change is facilitated by understanding people's mental models and involving them in the process. In short, the learning community believes that the only change that is opposed is one that is imposed.[3]

ENDNOTES

1 James Surowiecki, *The Wisdom of Crowds: Why the Many are Smarter than the Few and How Collective Wisdom Shapes Business, Economics, Societies and Nations* (New York: Doubleday, 2004), xvii.

2 Harvey A. Robbins and Michael Finley, *The New Why Teams Don't Work: What Goes Wrong and How to Make it Right* (San Francisco: Berrett-Koehler, 2000), 13-14.

3 "Definitions of Leadership: Ten Worth Remembering" (2005) [article online]; available from http://www.legacee.com/Info/Leadership/Definitions.html; Internet.

CHAPTER FOUR

LEADERSHIP STYLES FOR THE LEARNING COMMUNITY

It is important to examine various leadership styles to determine what type of leadership is consistent with the values of a learning community. It may be helpful first to establish a definition that fits within the conceptual framework of a learning community and organization. Harry S. Truman was once quoted as saying, "My definition of a leader . . . is a man who can persuade people to do what they don't want to do, or do what they're too lazy to do and like it."[1] For the learning community, leadership must be both task-oriented and relationship-oriented.

The concept of leadership may be the most studied yet least understood concept in organizations today. Several well known authors have offered definitions. Warren Bennis, best-selling author in the field of leadership, defines leadership as "a function of knowing yourself, having a vision that is well communicated, building trust among colleagues, and taking effective action to realize your own leadership potential."[2] Peter Senge, author of the *The Fifth Discipline*, defines the role of leaders as "…designers, stewards and teachers. They are responsible for building organizations where people continually expand their capabilities to understand complexity, clarify vision and improve shared mental models—that is, they are responsible for learning."[3] John C. Maxwell, in his book the *21 Irrefutable Laws of Leadership*, offers a simple definition: "Leadership is influence - nothing more, nothing less."[4]

Most experts agree with Truman that, in the end, leadership is influencing someone to do something they probably would not do on their own. Leadership style is defined not only by the end result of influence, but also by the means it uses to achieve those results. Truman suggests the use of persuasion as the means of influence while Senge favors teaching in order to influence. Merriam-Webster's dictionary defines a leader as "a person who directs a military force or unit, or a person who has commanding authority or influence."[5] This definition implies a commanding authority as the means of influence.

Years of study on the subject of leadership has helped to put to rest many misconceptions about the qualifications of leaders. Before 1945, the most common approach to the study of leadership concentrated on required traits, suggesting that certain characteristics, such a physical energy or friendliness, were essential for effective leadership.[6] The underlying assumption was that only people who demonstrated these traits could lead. Even the absence of one or more of these traits excluded potential candidates from assuming the responsibilities of leadership. But after fifty years of study, researchers have failed to produce one specific personality trait or set of qualities that can be used to discriminate between leaders and non leaders.[7] The conclusions drawn from years of research refute the notion that leadership is a function of personality.

Another misconception about leadership that still exists is the idea that leaders are either task-oriented or relationship-oriented, never both. Between 1945 and the mid-1960s, studies focused on the attitudinal approaches to leadership. In 1957, Ralph Stogdill, author *of Bass and Stogdill's Handbook of Leadership*, directed a research project at Ohio State University that identified two dimensions of leadership: initiating structure and consideration. Initiating structure refers to a leadership behavior best described as the extent to which a leader is task-oriented, directing subordinate activities toward goal achievement. Consideration describes leadership behavior that is sensitive to subordinates, respecting their ideas and feelings and establishing mutual trust.[8] The Ohio State staff found that the initiating structure and the consideration dimensions were separate and distinct. A high score on one dimension did not necessitate a low score on the other.[9] In other words, a leader could be highly task-oriented while being sensitive to subordinates and respecting their ideas and feelings. The general conclusion of the study was that both consideration and initiating structure are important to effective leadership. Considerate leadership communication increases follower satisfaction while decreasing hostility and strife. Initiating structure is important in guiding and organizing the completion of tasks.[10] The learning community embraces this idea that effective leaders can be task oriented while being sensitive to subordinates.

Robert Blake and Jane Mouton, in their book *The Managerial Grid*, developed a leadership grid that identified five different types of leadership based on a concern for production and a concern for people. The five leadership types are:

1. *Impoverished Management.* This leader demonstrates a low concern for tasks and a low concern for relationships.
2. *Authority-Compliance.* This leader is highly concerned with the completion of task assignments but demonstrates little concern for personal relationships.
3. *Middle-of-the-Road Management.* This leader is adequately concerned with production and people.
4. *Country Club Management.* This leader is more concerned with interpersonal relationships than with the completion of tasks.
5. *Team Management.* This leader demonstrates a high concern for both production and people. [11]

The most effective leadership communication style, according to Blake, is team management. Organizations that have implemented this style have increased productivity and profitability, increased frequency of communication, and improved leader-follower relations.[12] Blake and Mouton argued that maximum leadership effectiveness occurs only when a leader who is highly concerned for production and people integrates both the human and task requirements of the job. The exclusively task-oriented manager tends to treat employees as machines to the detriment of employee commitment, growth, and morale. The exclusively people-oriented manager is viewed as running a country club to the detriment of productivity.[13] The learning community's view of leadership considers the most effective leaders are those who are both task-oriented and relationship-oriented. However, even though a leader may adopt a style that values task-oriented and relationship-oriented behavior, he or she may violate the values of the learning community by withdrawing relational behavior in certain situations, thereby manipulating its members.

Paul Hersey and Ken Blanchard, developers of the popular Situational Leadership II model, propose that a manager should be either task-oriented and sell subordinates on what to do or relational-oriented and participate with subordinates in joint-decision making. Situational leadership classifies the leader's behavior as either task or relational. Managers should also delegate decisions depending on the subordinate's task-related maturity, meaning their capacity, ability, education and experience, and their psychological maturity, meaning their motivation, self-esteem, confidence, and willingness to do a good job.[14] The leader responds with either or both of these approaches based on the follower's level of commitment and competence. Relational behavior includes two-way communication, listening, and encouragement. Task behavior directs the follower as to the specifics of the task. The Hersey-Blanchard situational model has been applied widely but has yet to receive much research support.[15]

Blake takes exception to the underlying theory of situational leadership. He states that ". . . it is possible to tell a subordinate what to do, when to do it, how to do it, and so forth, and upon compliance give him socio-emotional rewards. The subordinate does no thinking only execution, and in return for compliance, gains acceptance. The combination is paternalism in its clearest form."[16] Even though the underlying assumption on the importance of these two behavior types is consistent with the learning community, the withdrawal of emotional support would not be consistent with the concept of supporting each other like friends. There is no room for paternalism or manipulation in a learning community. Thinking is the responsibility of every member, not the sole property of management.

When the balance between task-oriented and relationship-oriented behavior tilts toward the relationship, organizations lose their sense of mission. Paul Borden, executive minister of the American Baptist Churches of the West, finds that many churches are too focused on their internal relationships and have failed to focus externally on the mission of the Church. He states:

Most people enter congregations as consumers, seeking how a particular congregation will meet their needs. . . Individuals should expect congregations to have great worship, good teaching, groups where people can make friends and more. However, if this is all the people are given, the leadership of the congregation is pandering to their consumer mentality. . . The reason leadership wants to keep people coming is so they will be challenged to participate in the mission and vision of changing a community by making more disciples for Jesus Christ.[17]

The solution is to maintain the balance between caring for the flock and focusing on the mission of the Church. He continues, "In fact, performance is often seen as a negative value in judicatories since it makes the less effective family members feel guilty. . . Maintaining relative harmony in the family has become a priority over accomplishing the mission God has set out for congregations."[18]

In the New Testament, Paul and Barnabas were confronted with a difficult choice between mission and relationship. On Paul's first missionary journey, John Mark had abandoned Paul and returned home. As Paul prepared for his second journey, John Mark signed up for the trip. But the apostle refused to take him along because of his previous failure. The mission or task was too important to risk having John Mark bail out again. Barnabas, on the other hand, wanted to continue the relationship with John Mark. As a result, Paul and Barnabas decided to split up. Paul left on his second missionary journey and Barnabas sailed off with John Mark to Greece. Both the task and the relationship were preserved when John Mark returned to redeem himself with Paul by serving the mission of the Church later in his ministry.[19]

Theory X & Y

A popular misconception still prevalent today is the idea that leaders need to use command and control methods because followers are irresponsible behavior. In the late 1950s, Douglas McGregor, a professor of management at Massachusetts Institute of Technology, attempted to examine how a set of assumptions influences the behavior of managers. In his book, *The Human Side of Enterprise*, he identifies two basic approaches to supervision: Theory X management and Theory

Y management. Theory X managers believe the average person dislikes work and will avoid exerting effort whenever possible. These managers must direct, control and force workers to perform their jobs. Theory Y managers assume work is pleasant and a source of personal satisfaction. Instead of using threats, punishment and direct supervision to obtain compliance, these managers believe pride and personal commitment are sufficient to ensure quality work performance. This approach emphasizes individual commitment by recognizing both individual and organizational needs.[20] Theory X managers who believe workers are lazy or stupid will find it very difficult to empower workers to take on increasing responsibility. They would probably not take the time to develop or challenge employees. Instead, when this leader believes workers need to be supervised, he or she will find ways to control them. However, if grown-ups are treated like children, they tend to act like them. The psychology of control is a self-fulfilling prophecy.[21]

Leaders in a learning community and organization are Theory Y managers. Their assumptions about people are based on mental models that have been developed from years of personal and professional experience. Mental models are not permanent fixtures in a person's mind, but are subject to change through examination and new experiences. Contrary to popular belief, old dogs *can* learn new tricks. Or in this case, they can learn new ways of thinking.

Rensis Likert, in his book *New Patterns of Management*, discovered that high-producing supervisors "make clear to their employees what the objectives are and what needs to be accomplished and then gives them freedom to do the job."[22] He found that general, rather than close, supervision tended to be associated with high productivity. As a result of behavioral research studies of several organizations, Likert implemented organizational change programs in various industrial settings. These programs were intended to help organizations move from Theory X to Theory Y assumptions. In his studies, Likert found that the prevailing management styles of organizations can be depicted on a continuum from system one through system four. System one is a task-oriented, highly structured authoritarian management style, and system four is a relational-oriented management style based on teamwork, mutual trust, and confidence. Systems two and three are intermediate stages between the two extremes which closely approximate Theory X and Theory Y assumptions. He found almost without exception that the managers with the highest productive departments were rated closer to system four than the low producing departments. In addition to increases in productivity, manufacturing costs decreased 20 percent, turnover was cut almost in half, and morale rose considerably.[23] Theory Y managers fit well in the learning community because they believe people are capable of doing great things, provided they receive adequate information, authority, resources and accountability to be fully empowered.

Members of the learning community who hold Theory X assumptions can learn to change their assumptions to Theory Y. Giving up one's mental model may be a very difficult proposition for some managers. Their Theory X assumptions about workers may be the result of years of professional experience. Mental models are not permanent fixtures in a person's mind; they can be changed through examination and through new experiences. It takes commitment and willingness to be vulnerable. Peter Senge states, "Few leaders understand the depth of commitment required to build a learning organization. In practice, it is disorienting and deeply humbling because our old mental models were the keys to our confidence and competence. To be a real learner is to be ignorant and incompetent. Not many top executives are up for that." He continues, "Giving up control is very difficult, but it's virtually impossible if you have no idea of what you might get in its place. So, the safety required for learning might revolve around having some positive image of the future—something exciting enough for people to say, "I'd be willing to sacrifice to achieve that."[24] Developing a safe environment so people can be vulnerable to new learning is a key component of the learning community.

People are often put into leadership positions because they have the experience of being a leader in other settings, even if their styles may not fit with the organization's vision and values. Case in point: General George Patton, with his many years of experience in the military, probably would not have fit well in a learning organization that provided a level playing field and that invited people to contribute to the organization's vision. His leadership style would have been too authoritative to be effective in this type of organization. However, leaders who have experience within the U.S. Army Special Forces may be more suitable because of their ability to learn from difficult situations and respond accordingly without specific direction from their superior. This kind of special training allows a person to think independently and with the team while staying focused on the mission.

Incompatible Leadership Styles

Ken Blanchard says the most popular management approach today is seagull management. "These undisciplined managers are never around until you make a mistake and then they fly in, make a lot of noise, dump on everyone, and then fly out."[25] Needless to say, seagull management would not be conducive with the values of a learning community. Other types of leadership styles would be equally detrimental to empowering people while building community. Three such styles are authoritative, transactional and charismatic leadership.

Authoritative Leadership. Authoritative leaders maintain strict control over followers by using commands, direction, intimidation and reprimand as the primary means to accomplish assigned goals. They create distance between themselves and their followers as a way to emphasize role distinctions. Many authoritarian leaders are Theory X leaders who believe that followers will not function effectively without direct supervision. These leaders possess positional power; they are the center of focus. Wisdom and direction resides with them, not the followers. Authoritarians know what needs to be done and believe the follower is just an extension of his or her intent. The subordinate's response to the leader is compliance based on fear. The typical responses from these types of followers are Yes or Yes, Sir.

This style of leadership runs contrary to the values of a learning community and a learning organization. Friends do not support each other in this manner. Nor do they use fear to control each other. Partnerships with this type of leadership would not last long because followers are not empowered to use their abilities in a way that fosters commitment and ownership in the organization. There is no shared vision because the leader's vision is either told or sold to the follower. As long as followers pay lip service to the vision, the authoritarian leaders are satisfied. Authoritative leaders are not willing to share power for a variety of reasons but primarily because they may find their identity in their ability to manipulate and control people.

In contrast, in a learning organization the focus is shifted away from the leader and directed toward the follower. The learning community is led by servant leaders who are primarily concerned with raising the capacity of each member so they can make a greater contribution to the goals of the group. The learning community believes that followers are valuable and have knowledge that can benefit the organization. Power and wisdom are not the exclusive property of the leader.

Bernard Bass, in his *Handbook of Leadership*, cites two studies on the subject of power and leadership. One study noted that men with a high power motive displayed more instability in their interpersonal relations, had more arguments, were more impulsive, and engaged in more competitive sports. The second study obtained similar outcomes indicating that individuals with a high power motivation tended to inhibit group discussions more than did those with a low power motivation. Individuals with a high motivation for power also brought fewer facts and proposals that were available to them exclusively into the discussion. As a consequence, fewer alternatives were considered and the quality of decisions was lower from groups led by such individuals.[26] In a learning community, much of the power is disbursed to the group. Anything that disrupts the safe learning environment is eliminated.

Transactional Leadership. Transactional leaders use rewards as a means of controlling their followers. They use interactive goal setting and contingent personal and material reward and reprimands to influence the behavior of subordinates. In essence, the power is in the reward. Followers become calculators of how to get the reward, and they will comply as long as the reward is fulfilling and satisfying. Thus, the source of wisdom and direction belongs to the leader, not the followers.

Transactional leadership is a classic, time-honored leadership type found in the corporate world.[27] The television program *The Apprentice* provides a good example of transactional leadership. In the show, young men and women try to impress Donald Trump so they can avoid the contingent consequence of having Mr. Trump tell them, "You're fired." Trump may have a difficult time functioning in a learning community. This type of leader-follower interaction has often been explained as a social exchange. Bass describes the rules for contingent reinforcement in the "one minute manager's" game plan:

First, obtain the subordinates agreement with the goal (including the appropriate behavior for achieving it), and check the subordinate's behavior to see whether it matches the agreed on goal. Second, if the goal is achieved, provide praise (contingent reward) as soon as possible–making sure it is specific to what the subordinate did right. It is also vital to indicate how the subordinate's action helps others and the organization. Third, if the subordinate's performance fails to match expectations, deliver a reprimand (contingent punishment) as soon as possible after the failure. Despite the reprimand, it must be added, you should continue to think well of the subordinate but not of his specific performance. Fourth, the subordinate's success may call for setting a new goal, and the subordinate's failure may require a review and clarification of the old goal.[28]

But in a learning community, friends would not reprimand each other. Their performance would be open to discussion. Reprimand would stifle open and honest communication. In a learning community, learning is rewarded and time and resources are allocated to facilitate learning.

Charismatic Leadership. Charismatic leaders are characterized by an ability to create a highly motivating and absorbing vision of the future. Senge states,

> Our conventional notions of leadership are embedded in myths of heroes—great individuals severed from their community who make their way through individual will, determination, and cleverness. While there may be much to admire in such persons, we believe that our attachment to individualistic notions of leadership may actually block the emergence of the leadership of teams, and ultimately, organizations and societies that can lead themselves. While we wait for the great leader who will save the day, we surrender the confidence and power needed to make progress toward learning organizations.[29]

Charismatic leadership is a predominantly a top-down influence process. The leader is the primary source of wisdom and direction. Their power is based on a capability to generate a commitment from the follower to the leader's vision and persona. Transformational leader is another term used to describe this kind of leadership because the leader often uses exhortation and inspirational persuasion to influence followers. These leaders attract enthusiastic sheep.[30] But in a learning community, the focus of leadership is on the follower because enthusiastic sheep too easily abdicate their power; they will always look for someone else to inspire them. This is most noticeable when parishioners with a consumer mentality hop from church to church, looking for new inspiration.

Leadership styles that center attention on the leader instead of the follower are not conducive to the values of the learning community. Leadership styles that focus on empowering followers to grow and develop are consistent with the concept of the learning community.

Compatible Leadership Styles

The following leadership styles do complement learning communities. These styles include super leadership, side-by-side leadership, partnering intelligence, coaching and servant leadership.

SuperLeadership. The SuperLeader is someone who helps others to lead themselves. This person is also known as an empowering leader. With this type of leader, the focus is mainly on the followers. Leaders become *super*, possessing the strength and wisdom of many persons by helping to unleash the abilities of the followers who surround them. The SuperLeader multiplies his or her strength through the strength of others. By encouraging follower initiative, self-confidence, individual goal-setting, positive opportunity thinking, and self-problem solving, the SuperLeader encourages others to take responsibility. The spotlight is then placed on the follower. Followers, in turn, tend to experience exceptional commitment and ownership of their work.[31] This type of leadership fits comfortably within the framework of a learning community because the center of focus is on the followers in order to unleash their abilities to facilitate self-leadership.

Side by Side Leadership. Dennis A. Romig, in his book *Side by Side Leadership,* states that he reviewed more than three thousand studies in preparation for his book. Romig considered only field studies involving leaders in real organizations, studies in which scientific measurements documented genuine improvement in performance. He cites the results of a number of these studies which are compatible to leadership conducive to a learning community. Out of the seven principles he mentions in this book, the principle of the two-way street urges two-way communication, participation and cooperation in order to increase involvement and commitment. A review of ten of these studies found that when team leaders, supervisors, and managers were trained to listen effectively, their subordinates became more productive. When leaders received only eight hours of training in interpersonal listening skills, the team members increased productivity by 10 percent.[32] Improving listening skills for each member of the learning community is part of building capability.

The principle of interacting incorporates the use of two-way coaching to enhance performance. In one study, supervisors were trained to facilitate structured, thirty-minute one-on-one meetings with their contributors as discussions between equals on how they could improve performance. The supervisors were taught to step outside their position of authority for the session to conduct the discussion as equals. The result was a 15 percent improvement in productivity, compared with control groups in which performance reviews were conducted in a traditional format with supervisors rating subordinates from a position of authority.[33] Two-way coaching is another skill important to the effectiveness of the learning community.

Romig's principle of structured participation is accomplished when every member of the team and organization participates in implementing decisions and setting goals, and when everyone works together to achieve those goals. People are allowed to combine knowledge and experience in order to select the best ideas for improving performance. Leaders who share their knowledge side by side are more productive than those who do not.[34] A flat organizational structure allows for the free flow of information without information being the sole possession of people in positions of authority. Similarly, the principle of transferred authority empowers workers to make the improvements they see in their work area without waiting for upper management approval. This allows the benefits to be realized faster. Romig states that, in all of the research presented, the conclusions are clear: "When leadership is shared and mutual, workers are more innovative. They get the work done faster and at less cost."[35]

Partnering Intelligence. Steven Dent, author of *Partnering Intelligence*, uses this term to determine how well people can build relationships and cultivate trust while accomplishing predetermined tasks in an alliance with someone else. His Partnership Continuum provides a framework for partners to review and plan for the two major components, the task and the relationship, needed for successful partnerships. Partnerships don't just happen. They are designed. Because of this, Dent developed an assessment that identifies certain traits and skills that lead to successful partnerships. These traits and skills are comparable to those necessary for a successful learning community, and include: (a) looking to the future with a clear vision; (b) welcoming change; (c) creatively resolving conflicts and solves problems; (d) valuing interdependence; (e) creating trust through actions and words; and (f) openly self-disclosing information and giving feedback. The following characteristics can doom a partnership to failure: (a) relying on past history for decision making; (b) maintaining status quo while resisting change; (c) desiring to win conflicts; (d) valuing independence; (e) having a low trust of others; and (f) keeping information to self.[36]

Robert Kaplan and David Norton, co-authors of the *Balanced Score Card,* state that "Employees want to know where they fit within the organization and how they can contribute to helping it achieve its mission and objectives. Furthermore, leaders now recognize that their strategies, however brilliantly they may be formulated, will be successful only if everyone in the organization understands the strategy and helps to implement it. . . Rather than use measurement to control employees, leaders use strategy maps and Balanced Scorecards to communicate a vision for the future. . ."[37] In a learning community, each member takes part in the process of developing a shared vision, thereby making communication easier.

Elizabeth and Gifford Pinchot, who have more than thirty years of experience in executive coaching and consulting, state that "an organization is largely made up of people and their relationships with each other. . . The highest quality relationships are those of partnership, mutual support, and mutual respect for autonomy, not those in which one party dominates another. . . The explosive growth of the executive coaching industry, which often helps individual contributions improve their relationship skills, illustrates the depth of the gap between the supply and the demand for leaders with partnering skills."[38] Strong relationships are the foundation of the learning community.

Ken Blanchard, author and coauthor of more than thirty books including best-seller *The One Minute Manager,* states, "I think people want to be magnificent. It is the job of the leader, through partnering for performance, to bring out that magnificence in people and to create an environment in which they feel safe and supported and ready to do the best job possible in accomplishing key goals. . . Leaders must move from the command-and-control role of judging and evaluating to a role of ensuring accountability through supporting, coaching and cheerleading."[39] Performance is one of the highest priorities. Moving from a command-and-control style of leadership to a coaching style fits well into the design of a learning community.

Russ S. Moxley and John Alexander from The Center for Leadership and Ethics at Greensboro College suggest an alternative to individual leadership: leadership-as-partnership. They state, ". . . Partnership suggests the basic idea of men and women coming together to accomplish the leadership tasks—they create a shared vision, they work together to build commitment to and maintain alignment with the vision, and they use the skills and energies of all partners to handle change and deal with adaptive challenges. . . In partnerships, the source of a vision is the relationship; vision emerges from the reciprocity, from the give-and-take, of a relationship."[40] Shared vision, commitment, and interdependence are all values held by the learning community.

James M. Kouzes and Barry Posner, best-selling authors, state that "If the goal is superior performance, the winning bet will be on cooperation over competition and individualistic achievement every time. . . Pursuing excellence is a collaborator's game." They continue with the requirement for leadership by saying, "Leadership is more essential—not less—when collaboration is required. To succeed at collaboration, a leader must be able to skillfully create a climate of trust, facilitate positive interdependence, and support face-to-face interactions."[41] Cooperation, trust, and interdependence are all vital to the learning community.

Judy Rosenblum, chief operating officer of Duke Corporate Education, and Cheryl Oates, the corporation's co-director, alert people to the difficulty of trying to be a learning leader as partner. They state,

"Not only must leaders be able to create new meaning in their own community, but they must also successfully negotiate that meaning with others. Leaders need to be effective partners if they are to be the architects and orchestrators of a disconnected, but aligned, collaboration of entities and individuals with common interests."[42] The deepest level of commitment meets people's need for meaning and purpose in their lives.

Bob Nelson, author of the best-selling book *1001 Ways to Reward Employees*, believes the use of coercion, fear, and the threat of punishment do not work that well in most organizations today. He states in a separate article, "Most employees start new jobs excited about doing their best. Yet somehow, for many employees the excitement of the job quickly wears off. I believe this is due more than anything else to how employees are treated by their managers on a daily basis." [43] His advice to get the best effort from others is not accomplished by lighting a fire beneath them, but by building a fire within them. Building the fire within people in a learning community is facilitated by increasing their capabilities and aligning their personal vision with the vision of the organization.

James Belasco, executive coach and best-selling author of the *Flight of the Buffalo*, sees today's leader as a coach—a partner who helps transport people to higher and higher levels of personal and professional fulfillment. He proposes that, "Partner—leader—coaches help develop people to be more than they imagine they can be. They are the ear to listen, a smile to encourage, a word to reinforce, and some sage advice to consider."[44] Developing people is a primary responsibility of leadership in a learning community.

Coaching. Coaching is unlocking a person's potential to maximize their own performance.[45] Several experiments provide evidence that, as expected, coaching can improve leadership performance. Bass cites a study that compared ten control groups with approval of the leader "as is" after the first session, and ten groups with early coaching of the leader. Both observers and followers reported significant changes in leader attitudes toward those who were coached.[46] Improved performance and greater human relations are key ingredients of a learning community.

The Center for Creative Leadership, the world's largest institution devoted exclusively to leadership research and education, has identified three aspects of the formal coaching process: (a) relationship—the context within which the coaching occurs, (b) assessment, challenge and support (ACS)—the core elements of the leader development model, and (c) results—the visible outcomes that the coaching process is focused on achieving.[47] Relationship and results are important to successful coaching and effective learning communities. Robert E. Logan and Sherilyn Carlton propose a coaching model with the following five steps:

1. *Relate.* Establish rapport, mutual respect and trust. Being able to relate includes maintaining mutual respect and trust.
2. *Reflect.* Gain a deeper understanding of identified issues. Reflection allows for a deeper understanding of present issues.
3. *Refocus.* Clarify vision, brainstorming possible solutions and action planning.
4. *Resource.* Identify existing resources and explore new resources.
5. *Review.* Develop an action plan, process and coaching relationship evaluation.[48]

James Flaherty, author of *Coaching: Evoking Excellence in Others*, identifies the goals of generative coaching as long-term, sustainable excellent performance that is both self-correcting and self-generating. He states, "Most attempts to improve 'human resource' practices fall into the category of 'single loop learning.' That is it takes place without challenging the basic premises of the accepted paradigm. Generative Coaching is the result of 'double loop learning' in that it challenges the fundamental assumptions of existing theory and practice."[49] Generative coaching and the learning community are concerned with double-loop learning. Both examine the underlying assumptions to gain greater insight.

Servant Leadership. Robert Greenleaf, author of the book *Servant As Leader*, described the concept in this way:

The servant-leader is servant first. . . It begins with the natural feeling that one wants to serve, to serve first. Then conscious choice brings one to aspire to lead. He or she is sharply different from the person who is leader first, perhaps because of the need to assuage an unusual power drive or to acquire material possessions. For such it will be a later choice to serve— after leadership is established. The leader-first and the servant-first are two extreme types. Between them there are shadings and blends that are part of the infinite variety of human nature.[50]

The difference manifests itself in the care taken by the servant to first make sure that other people's highest priority needs are being served. The best test, although difficult to administer, is to ask whether those served grow as persons. Do they, while being served, become healthier, wiser, freer, more autonomous, and more likely themselves to become servants? And, what is the effect on the least privileged in society; will they benefit, or at least, will they not be further deprived?[51] Senge states:

> The emergence of collective leadership does not mean that there are no "leadership positions" like CEO or general or president in learning organizations. Management hierarchies are often functional, but the clash of collective leadership and hierarchical leadership nonetheless poses a core dilemma for learning organizations. This dilemma cannot be reconciled given traditional notions of hierarchical leaders as the people "in control" or "in charge." This then implies that those "below" are not in control. A hierarchical value system then arises that, as Analog Devices CEO Ray Stata puts it, "holds the person higher up the hierarchy as somehow a more important being." Alternatively, the dilemma can become a source of energy and imagination through servant leaders, people who lead because they chose to serve one another and for a higher purpose.[52]

Paul Border clarifies the goal of servant leadership in the church when he states:

> Most teaching on servant leadership focuses more on servanthood than it does leadership. Pastors are called to serve the people by serving the vision and mission God has, and in doing that the people are served even better. People are called to lead sheep, not just care for them. The sheep serve the needs of the shepherd. The sheep are not an end unto themselves.[53]

The learning community is served well by servant leaders who serve the other members of the group while achieving something greater than themselves. Leadership in learning communities is shared.

Each person is equally responsible for the success of the community's learning. Leaders of learning communities are facilitators or guides. Guides make occasional comments on the journey, pointing out what is happening along the way. Guides also facilitate the emptying process by continually emptying themselves and requesting the same of the group.[54] M. Scott Peck offers the following insights into the role of leadership in community:

> Community building requires that those accustomed to leadership be genuinely willing to enter a state of helplessness. It demands that I empty myself of my need to talk, my need to help all the time, my need to be a guru, my desire to look like a hero, my quick and easy answers, my cherished notions. But a group can learn how to go into emptiness only when its leader is able to practice emptiness.[55]

In the New Testament, Jesus did not stop after he washed the feet of the disciples. Instead, he told them they should wash one another's feet. Jesus also confirmed the servant leadership model when he said, "The Son of Man did not come to be served, but to serve"[56]

ENDNOTES

1 "What is Leadership" (2005) [article online]; available from http://www. teal.org.uk/Leadership/ definition.htm; Internet.

2 Peter M Senge, *The Fifth Discipline: The Art and Practice of the Learning Organization* (New York: Doubleday, 1990), 340.

3 John Maxwell, *21 Irrefutable Laws of Leadership* (Nashville: Thomas Nelson, 2002); quoted in "What is Leadership" (2005) [article online]; available from http://www.teal.org.uk/Leadership/ definition.htm; Internet.

4 Merriam-Webster's Collegiate Dictionary (2004), s.v. "leadership."

5 Paul Hersey, Kenneth H. Blanchard and Dewey E. Johnson, *Management of Organizational Behavior: Utilizing Human Resources*, 7th ed., (Upper Saddle River: Prentice-Hall, 1996), 101.

6 Eugene E. Jennings, "The Anatomy of Leadership," *Management of Personnel Quarterly* 1, no.1, (autumn 1961): 2-10.

7 Richard L. Daft, *Management*, 3rd ed., (Chicago: The Dryden Press, 1994), 484.

8 Hersey, Blanchard and Dewey, *Management of Organizational Behavior,* 105.

9 Michael Z. Hackman and Craig E. Johnston, *Leadership: A Communication Perspective* (Prospect Heights: Waveland Press, 1996), 46-47.

10 Robert R. Blake and Jane S. Mouton, *The Managerial Grid III: The Key to Leadership Excellence* (Houston: Gulf Publishing Company, 1985), 12-13.

11 R. R. Blake and A. A. McCanse, *Leadership Dilemmas—Grid Solutions* (Houston: Gulf Publishing Company, 1991), 29.

12 B. Bass, *Bass & Stogdill's Handbook of Leadership: Theory, Research & Managerial Applications,* 3rd ed. (New York: The Free Press, 1990), 483-485.

13 Ibid., 488-489.

14 Ibid., 494.

15 Robert R. Blake and Jane S. Mouton, "Grid Principles Versus Situationalism: A Final Note," *Group and Organizational Studies* 7, no. 2 (June 1982), 211-215.

16 Paul Borden, *Hit the Bullseye: How Denominations Can Aim the Congregation At the Mission Field* (Nashville: Abingdon Press, 2003), 98.

17 Ibid., 25-26.

18 Acts 15:36-40 NIV.

19 Douglas McGregor, *The Human Side of Enterprise* (New York: McGraw-Hill, 1960), 33-57.

[20] Kimball Fisher, *Leading Self-Directed Work Teams: A Guide to Developing New Team Leadership Skills* (New York: McGraw-Hill, 1993), 85.

[21] Rensis Likert, *New Patterns of Management* (New York: McGraw-Hill, 1961) 103.

[22] Ibid., 7.

[23] Peter Senge, "Learning Leaders" *Executive Excellence* 16, no. 11, (November 1999): 12-13.

[24] Scott Blanchard and Madeleine Homan, *Leverage Your Best, Ditch the Rest* (New York: HarperCollins, 2004), x.

[25] Bass. *Bass & Stogdill's Handbook of Leadership*, 132.

[26] Charles C. Manz and Henry P. Sims Jr., *The New SuperLeadership: Leading Others to Lead Themselves* (San Francisco: Berrett-Koehler, 2001), 41.

[27] Bass, *Bass & Stogdill's Handbook of Leadership*, 319.

[28] Peter M. Senge and Fred Kofman, "Communities of Commitment: The Heart of Learning Orgnanizations," *Organizational Dynamics* 22, no. 2, (autum 1993): 2-5.

[29] Manz and Sims Jr., *The New SuperLeadership*, 40-47.

[30] Ibid., 45.

[31] Dennis A. Romig, *Side by Side Leadership: Achieving Outstanding Results Together* (Marietta: Bard Press, 2001), 30-33.

[32] George Graen, Michael A. Novak, and Patricia Sommerkamp, "The effects of leader-member exchange and job design on productivity and satisfaction: Testing a dual attachment model." *Organizational Behavior and Human Performance* 30 (1982): 109-131.

[33] Daniel Goleman, *Emotional Intelligence: Why It Can Matter More Than I.Q.* (New York: Bantam Books, 1994), 161-162.

[34] Romig, *Side by Side Leadership*, 21.

[35] Stephen M. Dent, *Partnering Intelligence: Creating Value for Your Business by Building Strong Alliances* (Palo Alto: Davis-Black Publishing, 1999), 22.

[36] Robert Kaplan and David Norton, "Use the Balanced Scorecard to Partner with Strategic Constituents" in *Partnering: The New Face of Leadership*, eds. Larraine Segil, Marshall Goldsmith, and James Belasco. (New York: AMACOM Books, 2003), 10.

[37] Elizabeth Pinchot and Gifford Pinchot "Leading Organizations into Partnership" in *Partnering: The New Face of Leadership*, eds. Larraine Segil, Marshall Goldsmith, and James Belasco. (New York: AMACOM Books, 2003), 44.

[38] Ken Blanchard "Leadership Partnering for Performance Using Situational Leadership" in *Partnering: The New Face of Leadership*, eds. Larraine

Segil, Marshall Goldsmith, and James Belasco. (New York: AMACOM Books, 2003), 59.

[39] Russ S. Moxley and John R. Alexander, "Leadership-as-Partnership" in *Partnering: The New Face of Leadership,* eds. Larraine Segil, Marshall Goldsmith, and James Belasco. (New York: AMACOM Books, 2003), 75.

[40] James M. Kouzes and Barry Z. Posner, "Leaders Must Build Cultures of Collaboration" in *Partnering: The New Face of Leadership,* eds. Larraine Segil, Marshall Goldsmith, and James Belasco. (New York: AMACOM Books, 2003), 88.

[41] Judy Rosenblum and Cheryl Oates, "The Learning Leader as Partner" in *Partnering: The New Face of Leadership,* eds. Larraine Segil, Marshall Goldsmith, and James Belasco. (New York: AMACOM Books, 2003), 97.

[42] Bob Nelson, "Rub Somebody the Right Way" in *Partnering: The New Face of Leadership,* eds. Larraine Segil, Marshall Goldsmith, and James Belasco. (New York: AMACOM Books, 2003), 128.

[43] James Belasco "The Leader as Partner-Coach and People Developer" in *Partnering: The New Face of Leadership,* eds. Larraine Segil, Marshall Goldsmith, and James Belasco. (New York: AMACOM Books, 2003), 240.

[44] Timothy Gallwey, *The Inner Game of Tennis*, (New York: Random House, 1986), 23.

[45] Bass, *Bass & Stogdill's Handbook of Leadership*, 834.

[46] Sharon Ting and E. Wayne Hart, "Formal Coaching," in *The Center for Creative Leadership Handbook of Leadership Development*, 2nd ed., eds. Cynthia D. McCauley, Ellen Van Velsor. (San Francisco: John Wiley & Sons, 2004), 117.

[47] Robert E. Logan and Sherilyn Carlton, "Coaching 101" [article online]; available from http://coachnet.org/admin/files/upload/coachmodel.pdf; Internet.

[48] James Flaherty *Coaching: Evoking Excellence in Others* (Woburn: Butterworth-Heineman, 1999), 4, 198-214.

[49] Robert Greenleaf, *Servant As Leader* (1970); quoted in "What is Servant-Leadership," [article online]; available from http://www.greenleaf.org/leadership/servant-leadership/What-is-Servant-Leadership.html; Internet.

[50] Ibid.

[51] Senge and Kofman, "Communities of Commitment," 5-23.

[52] Borden, *Hit the Bullseye, How Denominations Can Aim the Congregation at the Mission Field* (Nashville: Abingdon Press, 2003), 22.

[53] Stephanie Ryan, "Emergence of Learning Communities" *Community Building: Renewing Spirit & Learning in Business,* ed. Kaximierz, Gozdz (San Francisco: New Leaders Press, 1995), 92.

[54] M. Scott Peck, *The Different Drum: Community Making and Peace* (New York: Simon & Schuster, 1987), 117.

[55] John 13:14 NIV; Matt, 20:28 NIV.

[56] Chris Argyris and Donald A. Schon, *Organizational Learning II: Theory, Method and Practice* (New York: Addison-Wesley Publishing Company, 1996), 187.

CHAPTER FIVE

THE LEARNING ORGANIZATION

As stated earlier, the antithesis of a learning community is exclusivity. Thus far, this study of the learning community process has concentrated on the effort to fit a small group of people into the leadership of an organization typically occupied by one person, the chief executive officer. This building process creates a small tight knit group of people committed to something greater than themselves. They learn to communicate effectively while examining their internal view of the world. They develop new ways of interacting and supporting each other the way friends do. They are empowered through the sharing of authority, resources, information and accountability. The learning community requires each person to walk the talk. Once a group has transformed themselves into a functional learning community, it will be necessary to transform the entire organization into a learning organization. All values held by the learning community are also core values of the learning organization. The learning organization, like the learning community, is concerned with including as many people in the group as possible. To replace the function of one chief executive officer with a small group to the exclusion of the rest would be inconsistent with the values of a learning organization.

Each member of the original learning community has the responsibility to facilitate the transformation process with their subordinates. Instead of one core group at the top, transforming to a learning organization requires the community to become a network of learning communities. Creating new learning communities takes a great deal of commitment on the part of leadership. But the goal is to create an organization that will learn to interact with each other in a new way so that every person becomes capable of contributing to the success of the organization.

Researchers and authors have written volumes trying to describe a learning organization. Their accounts are similar to the parable of four blind men who came across an elephant. These blind men decided to feel the elephant to determine what sort of creature it was. One blind man felt the back leg of the elephant and said, "An elephant is like a tree." The second blind man felt the trunk and said, "An elephant is like a snake." The third blind man felt the tail and said, "An elephant is like a rope." The fourth blind man was afraid. He didn't feel the elephant at all. The three blind men who did feel the animal argued a long time about what an elephant was. Based on each personal experience, each one was right. Even though these researchers and authors could not agree on a uniform definition of a learning organization, they were able to come up with some guides for organizational structures, processes, and conditions needed to enable productive organizational learning. Some of these prescriptions include:

1. Organizational structures should be flat and decentralized.
2. Organizations should develop information systems that provide fast public feedback to everyone in the organization.
3. Organizations should create mechanisms of surfacing and criticizing implicit organizational theories of action.
4. Organizations should improve measures that clearly reflect performance.
5. Organizations should develop systems of incentives aimed at promoting organizational learning.
6. Acceptable ideologies must be associated with measures, such as total quality, continuous learning, excellence, openness, and boundary-crossing.[1]

Virginia Marsick and Karen Watkins, authors of *In Action: Creating the Learning Organization,* highlighted the enormity of this task when they explained that "a learning organization must capture, share, and use knowledge so its members can work together to change the way the organization responds to challenges. People must question the old, socially constructed and maintained ways of thinking. Learning must take place and be supported in teams and larger groups, where individuals can mutually create new knowledge. And the process must be continuous because becoming a learning organization is a never-ending journey."[2]

While researchers and practitioners continue to debate the complexity of the learning organization, companies like Analog Devices, TXI Chaparral Steel and Xerox Corporation have recognized the link between learning and continuous improvement and have begun to refocus their companies to take advantage of this connection. Companies like the Honda Motor Company, Corning, and General Electric also have become adept at translating new knowledge into new ways of behaving. These companies actively manage the learning process to ensure that it occurs by design rather than by chance.[3]

Watkins and Marsick focused on dimensions of the learning organization, which they defined as "one that learns continuously and transforms itself." They explain that "while individuals can initiate some changes on their own as a result of their learning, the organization must create facilitative structures, policies, and cultures to support learning in larger groups and throughout the organization."[4] Rather than focus on learning processes, an audit of the learning organization examines the dimensions, or primary characteristics, of the organization. Watkins and Marsick also identify seven dimensions of a learning organization. A learning organization, they argue, (a) creates continuous learning opportunities, (b) promotes dialogue and inquiry, (c) promotes collaboration and team learning, (d) empowers people to evolve a collective vision, (e) establishes systems to capture and share learning, (f) connects the organization to its environment, and (g) provides strategic leadership for learning.[5] These seven dimensions are important because they provide the characteristics to create a learning organization.

The following sections put into behavioral terms what these seven dimensions will look like when the transformation is complete. The assessment process to measure these characteristics will be discussed in more detail in chapter 9.

Creates Continuous Learning Opportunities

On the individual level, the learning organization creates continuous learning opportunities. People openly discuss their mistakes in order to learn from them, instead of being punished or trying to assign blame when things do not go as planned. Leaders model the capacity to discuss mistakes in order to identify skills they need for future work tasks. The organization also systematically identifies skills required to do specific jobs by conducting competency assessments. Training and hiring are then focused on the future needs of the organization. People help each other learn because the organization provides recognition and rewards for doing so. However, resources such as personal development funds, resource libraries, and clear procedures to authorize learning activities are available for added support. Leaders also coach and mentor one another. People are given time to support learning by forming study groups that design work processes, which will, in turn, include reflection and learning.

In short, people view problems in their work as an opportunity to learn, which may include structuring trial and error into the actual work process. People are rewarded for learning. Tangible rewards such as tying pay increases to knowledge or educational level, building learning incentive into individual development plans, and offering tuition reimbursement all encourage learning.

Promotes Dialogue and Inquiry

Learning organizations promote inquiry and dialogue so that employees can give open and honest feedback to each other instead of suppressing the open exchange of ideas. Lack of feedback makes it difficult to understand expectations or to change behavior to meet expectations. In a learning organization, time is set aside to reflect and provide feedback at the end of meetings. People listen to each others' views before speaking and can actually finish their sentences before someone else comments. Everyone is encouraged to share ideas and perceptions even if they conflict with those of someone else. Active listening along with dialogue, skillful discussion and brainstorming are all valued skills. Employees are encouraged to ask why regardless of rank, as opposed to having to agree with a hierarchy that often suppresses the communication of quality ideas. Everyone is included in the decision-making processes, and there are anonymous suggestion systems that encourage leaders to model a willingness to be challenged. Whenever a person states his or her view, that person is also required to ask for feedback. This is where dialogue, skillful discussion, and active listening become necessary skills to invite challenge without personal threat. People in the organization treat each other with respect by not covering their competitiveness with false politeness. In this organization, people spend time building trust with each other as a means of overcoming a culture of fear. Leaders model a more collegial relationship with employees and help build trust by sharing their rationale behind difficult decisions. Team building sets the norm for trustworthy behavior.

Promotes Collaboration and Team Learning

The group level of the learning organization encourages collaboration and team learning, and as such, teams or groups then have the freedom to adapt their goals as needed. In this organization, team or group members are treated as equals, regardless of rank, culture, or other differences. People can express their views without having the hierarchy restrict the free flow of ideas and information. As a result, everyone is fully and equally involved in discussions and decisions. Roles within the group are rotated so that everyone has a chance to develop leadership skills. In this organization, groups focus on the task and on how well the group is working. They spend time developing relationships since these stronger relationships have been proven to impact productivity. They also spend time training in group dynamics. Team building reduces conflict that impedes productivity. In a learning organization, groups revise their thinking as a result of discussions or information collected. They are also able to break out of mental frameworks that tie them to past strategies and goals. In this organization, teams or groups are rewarded for their achievements as a team, not for individual accomplishment. But members are also acknowledged and rewarded for their contribution to the group. The organization ensures the appropriate consideration of a group's recommendations. As a result of this arrangement, teams or groups are then confident that the organization will act on those recommendations.

Empowers People to Evolve a Collective Vision

The learning organization recognizes people for taking initiative. Employees are provided with parameters for their work and are expected to establish goals, determine strategies, and make decisions. People are given choices in their work assignments and are encouraged to step outside the box. If possible, flexible work arrangements are offered. The learning organization invites people to contribute to the organization's vision, and because the development of vision and strategy is decentralized, employees are expected to implement those visions. This is because people who are involved in setting the vision are more motivated to implement it. Collaborative visioning is facilitated through strategy-focused task forces and staff meetings focused on strategic direction. People then have control over the resources they need to accomplish their work without having to go through layers of management for permission. Decentralized decision making allows adequate access to those resources. Decentralization is not risk aversive to an extreme, but supports employees who take calculated risks and who show a willingness to experiment with new ideas, ideas that are promising though not clearly proven. Decentralization builds alignment of visions across different levels of work groups by coordinating their work with other parts of the organization. Joint work groups and access to the work plans other groups help build this alignment.

Establishes Systems to Capture and Share Learning

At the organizational level, the organization creates systems to capture and share learning. Two-way communication is used on a regular basis in the form of suggestion systems, electronic bulletin boards, or town hall or open meetings. This provides more opportunities for widespread sharing of information. People can receive needed information quickly and easily because they have access to the technology and the skills to use it effectively. Knowledge networks and communities of practice are established. In this organization, an up-to-date database of employee skills is maintained in order to easily access employee skills and knowledge. Systems are also created to measure gaps between current and expected performance. The Balance Scorecard, a system discussed further in chapter 9, provides an effective system of measurement to keep track of organizational changes. Leadership makes learned information available to all employees through database documenting of situations, actions and consequences. The organization also adopts assessments that measure the results of time and resources spent on training. The learning organization does not rely on perceptions or intentions to evaluate training at the individual or organizational level, but instead uses this data to examine the performance and the costs associated with the results.

Connects the Organization to its Environment

Learning organizations connect the organization to its environment. In doing this, the organization helps employees balance work and family by providing programs that address a work-life balance. Programs may include family leave benefits, support groups for families in trouble, employee assistance programs, or training for managers in supporting the families of their employees. People are encouraged to think globally by paying attention to the potential global effect on their business. The organization encourages everyone to bring the views of customers into the decision-making process by conducting customer surveys or focus groups, increasing direct customer contact, analyzing competitors, and engaging in scenario planning to imagine and meet multiple customer needs. Leadership considers the impact of decisions on employee morale by conducting employee climate or opinion surveys or employee focus groups prior to reaching a major decision. Discussions are held to follow up on decisions taken. The organization also works together with the outside community to meet mutual needs by becoming involved in local communities. This includes meeting with key community leaders and coordinating joint efforts such as fund raising. Employees are encouraged to find answers when solving problems through the establishment of cross-functional teams to facilitate organization-wide problem solving.

Provides Strategic Leadership for Learning

Learning organizations provide strategic leadership for learning. Leaders generally support requests for learning opportunities and training by encouraging employees to pursue goals that will improve their capabilities. Leaders also discuss development plans and opportunities and make information and resources available for development. They share up-to-date information with employees about competitors, industry trends, and organizational directions by conducting employee information meetings, posting environmental scanning information, and using marketing programs to gather data. Leaders empower others to help carry out the organization's vision by decentralizing decision making and empowering individuals or teams to take actions that support the organization's vision. In this organization, leaders also mentor and coach those they lead, instead of using direction and discipline. Leaders are taught coaching and mentoring strategies and are rewarded for using them. Measurements of leadership competency include these skills. Leaders continually look for opportunities to learn instead of assuming they have all the answers. They are given a minimum time set aside each year for learning, holding leadership retreats, reading and discussing books, making leadership resources available on-line, and pursuing further education. They ensure that the organization's actions are consistent with its values, and hold other leaders accountable for modeling those values. They also regularly examine the implications of decisions to ensure consistency.[6]

Like the blind men trying to describe the elephant, mentioned at the beginning of this chapter, many authors and researchers have only been able to define the learning organization from their own perspective. But the best perspective allows the learning community to use these seven characteristics to shape the organization into a learning organization.

ENDNOTES

[1] Virginia Marsick and Karen Watkins, *In Action: Creating the Learning Organization* (Alexandria: American Society for Training Development, 1996), 4.

[2] David A. Garvin, "Building a Learning Organization" *Harvard Business Review* 71, no. 4, (July/August 1993), 19-29.

[3] Marsick and Watkins, *In Action: Creating the Learning*, 4.

[4] Virginia Marsick and Karen Watkins, *Dimensions of the Learning Organization Questionnaire* (Warwick: Partners for the Learning Organization, 1997) [online questionnaire]; available from http://www.partnersforlearning.com/instructions.html; Internet.

[5] Ibid.

[6] Deane Zell. "Organizational Change as a Process of Death, Dying and Rebirth" *Journal of Applied Behavioral Science* 39, no. 1, (March 2003): 73-96.

CHAPTER SIX

COPING WITH CHANGE

Change in many organizations emanates from the top of the organization and moves down the chain of command to the front line, usually in response to some perceived crisis. The front-line people have two choices available to them: (a) they can fail to recognize the crisis and continue working the way they always have, or (b) they can trust the judgment of top management and comply, hoping top management knows what they are doing. Most people respond somewhere between complacency and compliance. As an example, today people are increasingly becoming aware of the difference between junk food and healthy foods. My wife had been trying to make me eat healthy for years. But I, reluctant to change, continued my unhealthy eating habits just the same. Not until my doctor shared with me the results of my lab work did I finally begin to realize the sense of urgency. Similarly, this type of information sharing characteristic in a learning community facilitates the change process in an organization.

Difficulty of Change

For some people, change can trigger feelings of frustration, anger, helplessness and depression; and yet, these feelings have often been dismissed as a resistance to change. In a study funded by the Alfred P. Sloan Foundation to better understand the process of working through resistance to change in a professional bureaucracy, Deane Zell, an assistant professor of management at California State University-

Northridge, found that the process of change experienced by a physics department in a large public research university in response to a crisis that threatened its survival resembled the process of death and dying experienced by terminally ill patients. The physics professors progressed through five distinct stages that included denial, anger, bargaining, depression, and finally, acceptance. The process of change was not only painful, but it took almost two years before they reached the acceptance stage.[1]

Robert Quinn captures the distinction between incremental and deep changes by stating, "Incremental change is usually the result of a rational analysis and planning process. Deep change differs from incremental change in that it requires new ways of thinking and behaving. . . Most of us build our identity around knowledge and competence in employing certain known techniques or abilities. Making a deep change involves abandoning both and 'walking naked into the land of uncertainty.'"[2] This kind of deep change is more likely to take place in a learning community where people support each other like friends. In this safe environment, people have the opportunity to examine mental models to create new ways of thinking; whereas, in other group or team settings, having one's mental models criticized may be too threatening. Defensiveness and rationalization may interfere with "walking naked into the land of uncertainty."

Impeding Attitudes to Change

Peter Senge, in his article "Creating Change," identified ten distinct forces that oppose organizational change. There are three major phases of this process: initiating change, sustaining momentum, and redesigning the organization. The first four forces—time, help, relevance, and walking the talk—come into play when initiating change.

1. *Time.* "We don't have time for this stuff" is the prevailing attitude that impedes the change process. Trapped between the daily workload and aspirations to change the workplace, leaders quickly realize that even ideas that have broad appeal are never implemented because there is simply no time for people to engage in serious change efforts. The challenge for the learning community is to trust people to control their work and eliminate unnecessary work. Leaders who put time into

developing people around them will find themselves with more time available.

2. *Help.* "We have no help" or "We're wasting our time" is another impeding attitude when initiating change. Developing new learning capabilities takes time, persistence, and coaching from experienced people. If it were easy to develop capabilities, everyone would be doing it. The learning community may need additional help in the beginning, but after the group masters the concepts of dialogue, reflection and generative thinking, it should be self-sustaining. The members of the learning community build an internal capacity to be coaches for each other and for subordinates.

3. *Relevance.* "This stuff isn't relevant" is a prevailing mantra. Managers often think that because a change is relevant to them, the relevance is clear to others. If the change is not relevant, commitment is undermined. The learning community needs to build awareness among its leaders and to raise questions about the relevance of change initiatives to the group. Linking the changes to business results will help with raising the awareness of relevance.

4. *Walking the talk.* "They're not walking the talk" is a main observation that impedes change. Many people commit only if they have confidence in those advocating the change. If leaders are perceived as not walking the talk, the inconsistency will limit people's willingness to commit to any initiatives. The members of the learning community build credibility by demonstration, not by articulation. Each member actively solicits feedback from peers and coaches regarding the member's ability to live out the values of the organization.

The next three forces—fear and anxiety, measurement, and true believers and non-believers—come into play after early successes have been achieved and the problems of sustaining momentum arise.

5. *Fear and anxiety.* "This isn't good" describes the attitude impeding change when attempting to sustaining momentum. Anxiety arises because everyone fears making a mistake, showing ignorance, or hurting others. All change efforts can

induce fear because the change process may threaten long-held beliefs and attitudes. Fear may cause people to withdraw or to act defensively. The learning community sets the standard by openly discussing mistakes and assuring others that fear and anxiety are natural responses to a learning situation.

6. *Measurement.* "This stuff is not working" is a typical observation during this point in the change process. This challenge arises because some people expect to see improvement immediately. The learning community allows people to assess their own progress toward improvement. They realize that it takes time to see profound changes.

7. *True believers and non-believers.* Believers often think "We have the way" whereas non-believers think, "They are acting like a cult." Often, team members involved in innovative efforts split into believers and non-believers. This split need not escalate if the learning community respects people's inhibitions about change and cultivates open communication.

   The final three forces—governance, diffusion, and strategy and purpose—arise as the work gains credibility and challenges the organization's existing culture and practices.

8. *Governance.* "They (the powers that be) never let us do this stuff" can be a main impeding attitude during this phase. Innovative groups become caught up in issues of accountability and power. These issues may arise when members press for more autonomy, feeling they can make decisions on their own when they cross boundaries. The learning community incorporates accountability and the redistribution of power. Authority and power are transferred as soon as the person is capable of handling the responsibility.

9. *Diffusion.* "We keep reinventing the wheel" describes the frustration created when innovation remains within certain pockets in the organization without being shared. Learning communities meet this challenge by creating a climate that encourages risk-taking and by sharing what people have learned.

10. *Strategy and purpose.* "What are we here for?" is the main question at this point. This challenge requires rethinking the

strategy process. The strategic process in a learning community tries to include as many people in the room as possible so they can be a part of the planning process. Scenario planning is a useful tool at all levels of the organization.[3]

The Learning Community and the Stages of Change

John Kotter, in his book *Leading Change*, lays out an eight-stage prescription for change. Similar to Senge's three phases, Kotter breaks his stages into three parts. He devotes the first four steps in the transformation process to helping defrost a hardened status quo. Steps five through seven introduce many new practices. The last stage grounds the changes in the corporate culture.[4]

1. *Establishing a sense of urgency.* Establishing urgency is crucial to gaining needed cooperation. Transformations usually go nowhere when complacency is high because few people are even interested in working on the change problem. It is difficult to put together enough power and credibility to guide the effort when urgency is low. One of the goals of the learning community is to create or achieve something greater than themselves. This value does not allow for complacency to creep into the community. Kotter lists several reasons why complacency exists: (a) there is no highly visible crisis, (b) people rest on previous success, (c) low standards prevail, (d) employees focus on narrow functional goals, (e) internal planning and control systems are rigged, and (f) faulty internal feedback systems are used.[5] Leaders within the learning community must be able to create a strong sense of urgency by constantly raising the standards of performance without having to create a crisis to facilitate change.

2. *Creating the guiding coalition.* Creating a guiding coalition needs to be done with the right composition, level of trust, and shared objectives. No one individual is ever able to develop the right vision and eliminate all key obstacles on his or her own. Kotter lists four key characteristics to an effective guiding coalition: position power, expertise, credibility and leadership.
   To keep those left out from easily blocking progress, position power asks the question, Are enough key players on board, especially the main line managers? In order for change to

infiltrate the entire organization, every key player must be part of the learning community. Key people who could potentially block the change initiative must not be allowed to work independent of the learning community.

Expertise asks the question, Are the various points of view—in terms of discipline, work experience, nationality, and cultural background relevant to the task at hand—adequately represented so that informed, intelligent decisions can be made? The learning community must be able to identify a legitimate need for each member of the team. Those with specific expertise should be included in the community.

Credibility asks the question, Does the group have enough people with good reputations within the firm so that informed, intelligent decisions can be made? Key players should have good reputations to ensure credibility. If they do not, their behavior should be modified, or the need for their position in the organization should be reevaluated.

Leadership asks the question, Does the group include enough proven leaders to be able to drive the change process? Leadership styles must be in alignment with the values of the learning community. Certain leadership styles, such as authoritarian, charismatic, or transactional, may run contrary to effective leadership within a learning community. The balance between manager and leader will also become an important part of each member's development plan.

Creating trust is an important goal for a guiding coalition and a learning community. Trust is built through on- and off-site activities. Intellectual activities aimed at the head and bonding activities aimed at the heart are both important to building trust in the guiding coalition and the learning community. Leadership in the learning community emphasizes both relational and task-oriented behaviors because the community will spend a great deal of time face-to-face building relationships and solving problems together.

3. *Developing a vision and strategy.* In a change process, a good vision serves three important purposes: (1) it clarifies the general direction for change, (2) it motivates people to take action

in the right direction even if the initial steps are personally painful, and (3) it helps coordinate the actions of different people in a remarkably fast and efficient way.[6] The learning community is responsible for the joint development of a shared vision. Shared vision is emphasized because the typical process of the chief executive officer developing the vision and selling it to everyone else may be less effective in fostering ownership and commitment. The community develops a shared vision to which they all can commit, not just one that elicits compliance. Once they make a covenant with each other, they are each committed to a set of specific actions. As part of the process, members of the learning community solicit input and commitment from their constituents to determine if the vision passes the true test of any good vision. This determining test asks whether the vision is imaginable, desirable, feasible, focused, flexible and communicable.

4. *Communicating the vision of change.* There are several key elements in the effective communication of vision: simplicity, metaphor, multiple forums, repetition, leadership by example, explanation of inconsistencies, and two-way communications.[7] Each member of the learning community has the responsibility to create learning communities with their subordinates. This involves each person acting as a coach within the group. In addition to being the coach, each member also facilitates the community building process. This gives each member several opportunities to communicate the vision of change. Effective use of two-way communication and leadership by example are inherent within the values of a learning community.

5. *Empowering employees for broad-based action.* Empowering employees is accomplished by providing the training people need to effect change and by removing the obstacles so they can do more. Four of the biggest obstacles to empowerment are: structures, skills, systems, and supervisors. More successful ways in which to empower people to effect change are to communicate a sensible vision to employees, make structures compatible with the vision, provide the training employees need, align information and personnel systems to the vision, and to

confront supervisors who undercut needed change.[8] The goal of leadership in the learning community is to develop people to be fully capable of taking on as much responsibility as they can possibly handle. When individuals are capable, responsibility is transferred so they can contribute more to the organization.

6. *Generating short-term wins.* Short-term wins provide evidence that the sacrifices are worth it. Wins help justify greatly the short-term costs involved. Rewarding change with a pat on the back and after a lot of hard work gives positive feedback that builds morale and motivation. Wins help fine-tune vision and strategies, and short-term wins give the guiding coalition concrete data on the viability of their ideas. They also undermine the cynics and self-serving resisters because clear improvements in performance make it difficult for people to block needed change. Bosses are kept on board, and those higher in the hierarchy are provided with evidence that the transformation is on track. Wins build momentum and turn neutral members into supporters and reluctant supporters into active helpers.[9] Part of the increasing capability process includes making the learning community aware of the benefits of short-term wins.

7. *Consolidating gains and producing more change.* A successful, major change effort creates more change, not less. Because of this, the guiding coalition uses the credibility afforded by short-term wins to tackle additional and bigger change projects. Additional people are then brought in, promoted, and developed to help with all the changes. Senior people focus on maintaining the overall clarity of the shared purpose and on keeping the urgency level up. Managers from lower ranks in the hierarchy provide leadership for specific projects. In order to make change easier for the short and long term, managers identify unnecessary interdependencies to eliminate them.[10] The learning community must become aware of how to consolidate gains in order to produce more change.

8. *Anchoring new approaches in the culture.* The anchoring of change in a culture comes last because most alterations in norms and shared values come at the end of the transformation process. Successful new approaches usually sink into a culture only after

it is very clear that they are superior to old methods. Without verbal instruction and support, people are often reluctant to admit the validity of new practices. But if promotion processes are not changed to be compatible with the new practices, the old culture will reassert itself.[11]

Conclusion

The learning community facilitates the change initiative by involving as many people as possible in the process. The learning community becomes the guiding coalition that establishes a sense of urgency for everyone in the organization. They align personal visions with the vision of the organization, and they decide how they will contribute to the strategy of the organization. Leaders communicate the vision of change during community-building and coaching sessions with their subordinates. Leaders are charged with the responsibility of developing their people so they can assume new and challenging responsibilities. They generate short term wins and consolidate those wins to implement new changes within the organization.

ENDNOTES

1 Robert E. Quinn *Deep Change: Discovering the Leader Within* (San Francisco: Jossey-Bass, 1996), 3.

2 Peter M. Senge and Katrin H Kaeufer, "Creating Change" *Executive Excellence* 17, no. 10, (October 2000): 4-5.

3 John P. Kotter, *Leading Change* (Boston: Harvard Business School Press, 1996), 22.

4 John P. Kotter, "Kill Complacency" *Fortune* 13, no. 3, (August 5, 1996): 168.

5 John P. Kotter, "Leading by Vision and Strategy" *Executive Excellence* 14. no. 10, (October 1997): 15.

6 Kotter *Leading Change*, 90.

7 Ibid., 102.

8 Ibid., 123.

9 Ibid., 143.

10 Ibid., 157.

11 Dudley Weeks, *The Eight Essential Steps to Conflict Resolution: Preserving Relationships at Work, at Home, and in the Community* (New York: G. P. Putnam's Sons, 1992), 7.

CHAPTER SEVEN

CONFLICT RESOLUTION

The word conflict usually has a negative connotation and is often associated with a fight or some antagonistic state between people with opposing demands. In truth, conflict is neither positive nor negative; conflict is actually an outgrowth of diversity that can be utilized to clarify a relationship.[1]

Roger Fisher and William Ury, co-authors of the best-selling book *Getting to Yes*, offer some valuable advice to prevent conflict when they state, "However, the best time for handling people problems is before they become people problems. This means building a personal and organizational relationship with the other side that can cushion the people on each side against the knocks of negotiation. Knowing the other side personally really does help. Dealing with a classmate, a colleague, a friend, or even a friend of a friend is quite different from dealing with a stranger. The more likely you can turn a stranger into someone you know, the easier a negotiation is likely to become. The time to develop such a relationship is before the negotiation begins."[2]

In the learning community, people are asked to examine deeply held internal views of the world. This process will inevitably create conflict which, if not addressed properly, has the potential to destroy the community-building process so necessary to the success of creating a learning organization. The learning community takes to heart the authors' suggestion by attempting to build strong relationships before conflicts arise. The members of the learning community become a support for each other in the way real friends do. The goal of any conflict resolution method is to preserve relationships while appreciating the diversity of the group.

Ineffective Approaches to Conflict

While many of the following methods are popular, all of these approaches remain ineffective in conflict resolution.

The Conquest Approach. This approach is implemented when one person tries to weaken the other party in order to make his or her own strength greater. Power is used in negative and destructive ways where one person controls the other. One person is disempowered and becomes the loser. But this approach does nothing to improve the relationship. An example of this approach could include an overbearing husband who verbally abuses his wife through intimidation.

The Avoidance Approach. Here people expend their energy avoiding relationships with people who differ in values, ideas, lifestyle and other characteristics. This approach postpones dealing with conflict which only allows it to worsen. Avoidance denies parties the chance to clarify their relationship.

The Bargaining Approach. This approach sees conflict resolution as a game in which success and power are defined by how much one party can make the other party concede, either by coercing them or by forcing them to give up. This practice obscures the relative value of needs. Those who have closely observed American labor-management negotiations have suggested that the process tends to follow a general pattern. This process, repeated in most cases of contract negotiations, can be characterized as having three main parts: (1) establishing positions, (2) probing for strengths and weaknesses in the positions of each other, and (3) reaching a conclusion.[3]

The Band-Aid Approach. This approach is an attempt to provide a quick-fix solution in order to avoid conflict. It creates the illusion that the fundamental problems have been addressed. However, there can be no confidence in any process that does not provide a lasting improvement in the relationship. This approach disempowers all parties because it does not develop a process anyone can use effectively for future conflicts. My company once introduced a conflict resolution process that had the net result of a band aid approach. Whenever a manager became aware of a conflict situation, that manager would require the two parties to resolve the issue on their own. This procedure did not offer a resolution process that attempted to preserve the relationship. In effect, the message to both parties was, "Either you solve the problem or the manger will."

The Role-Player Approach. This approach avoids relating to others as people. Instead, people relate to each other only from a persona perspective: boss to employee, teacher to student, and parent to child. Those with lesser status and power usually will be further disadvantaged, ultimately disintegrating the relationship. This is an unfair relationship that cheats the conflict resolution process. The options for resolving conflicts are greatly restricted and, in turn, create an adversarial relationship.[4] This approach is often played out in the workplace where the supervisor relates to the subordinate from a position of authority and where the rules favor the supervisor's special position over the employee.

Experts Advice on Conflict Resolution

There are a number of books available to help resolve conflict. Dudley Weeks, in his book *The Eight Essential Steps to Conflict Resolution*, offers some helpful steps:

1. *Create an effective atmosphere.* The atmosphere has the potential to promote positive interaction. Creating an atmosphere for effective conflict resolution includes paying attention to personal preparation, the timing, the location, and the initial opening statements each party makes once they are together.

2. *Clarify perceptions.* Perceptions are the lenses through which people see themselves, others, their relationships, and the situations encountered. The conflict partnership process focuses on clarifying perceptions in three critical areas: the conflict, the self, and the conflict partner.

3. *Focus on individual and shared needs.* In relationships, the personal needs perceived by each individual should also consider the needs of the relationship. Conflicts often arise when needs are ignored or appear to be incompatible. Conflict partners must develop insights and skills pertaining to four sets of needs present in every relationship: personal needs, the partner's needs, relationship needs, and shared needs.

4. *Build shared positive power.* Every relationship involves power. Power consists of the attitudes, perceptions, beliefs, and behaviors that give people and groups the ability to perform effectively. The major task is to discover how the conflict partnership process uses the positive power of the individual, of the other partner, and of shared power.

5. *Look to the future; then learn from the past.* Because every relationship and every conflict has a past, present, and future, resolving conflicts effectively requires that partners deal with all three. Conflict partners begin by dealing with how the past can impede conflict resolution. Then they will look at the present and the future.

6. *Generate options.* Generating options can often break through the preconceived limitations brought into the conflict resolution process. Doing this provides choices from which specific steps to resolve conflicts and improve relationships can be agreed upon.

7. *Develop doables, the stepping-stones to action.* The critical task of this step is to implement those specific actions the parties in conflict can take to improve their relationship and resolve conflicts within the relationship.

8. *Make mutual-benefit agreements.* Effective and lasting mutual-benefit agreements must be built on clarified perceptions of the conflict, the partners involved in the conflict, and the specific steps each partner has agreed to take to improve the relationship.[5]

In their best-selling book *Getting to Yes*, Fisher and Ury state, "Any method of negotiation may be fairly judged by three criteria: It should produce a wise agreement if agreement is possible. It should be efficient. And it should improve or at least not damage the relationship between parties. (A wise agreement can be defined as one which meets the legitimate interests of each side to the extent possible, resolves conflicting interests fairly, is durable, and takes community interests into account.)"[6] Fisher and Ury propose a four step method to negotiations: (1) separate the people from the problem, (2) focus on interests, not positions, (3) invent options for mutual gain, and (4) insist on using objective criteria. Most methods for conflict resolution are implemented after the fact, after the conflict has escalated to the point where it has a negative impact on the work environment.[7]

Cooperation vs. Competition

Morton Deutsch in his book, *The Resolution of Conflict*, offers some suggestions on how to prevent conflict and initiate cooperation. In the process of building meaningful relationships with members of the learning community, many of these suggestions are already implemented. Deutsch states that it is useful to know something about the following: (a) the characteristics of the parties in conflict, (b) their values and motivations, (c) their aspirations and objectives, (d) their physical, intellectual, and social resources for waging or resolving conflict, (e) their beliefs about conflict and personal vision, and (f) their conception of strategy and tactics. During the group building process, members of the learning community conduct an audit of their values to see if there is potential for conflict between people who prioritize some values over others. They take the DISC personality inventory (discussed in chapter 2) that reveals the differences in decision-making styles and how they respond to change. They share their personal visions with the hope of aligning their vision with that of the organization. Deutsch suggests that it would also be useful to know something about their prior relationship to one another, including their attitudes, beliefs, and expectations about one another. This would also include knowing each one's perception of how they view each other, along with an understanding of the social environment in which the conflict occurs.[8]

Building relationships based on trust is one of the primary goals of a learning community. Members of the community become aware of each person's attitudes, beliefs and expectations of one another, including each one's belief about the other based on open and honest feedback. The social environment of a learning community is one where people support each other as friends. The environment encourages dialogue between members without personal threats or intimidation.

Creating an Environment of Cooperation

Creating an environment of cooperation within a learning organization rather than one of competition contributes to the prevention of conflict between members. In 1948, Deutsch conducted an experiment with Massachusetts Institute of Technology undergraduates enrolled in his introductory psychology course. One group was told their discussions of the human relations problem would be graded competitively while the other group was told they would be graded cooperatively. The results showed striking differences between the cooperative and competitive groups. The cooperative groups showed the following characteristics:

1. They were more effective at inter-member communication.
2. They were more friendliness, more helpful, and less obstructive to the discussion.
3. There was more coordination of effort, division of labor, orientation to task achievement, and orderliness in discussion. Therefore, they were more productive.
4. There was more feeling of agreement, similarity in ideas, and confidence in one's own ideas and in the value that other members attached to those ideas. [9]

Deutsch's findings demonstrate the significant differences between the processes involved in cooperation and competition. Communication in a cooperative process is characterized by open and honest dialogue; whereas communication in a competitive process is characterized by either misleading communication or a lack of it. A cooperative process tends to increase sensitivity to similarities and common interest while minimizing the salience of differences. It stimulates a convergence and conformity of beliefs and values. A competitive process tends to increase sensitivity to differences and threats while minimizing the awareness of similarities. The cooperative process leads to trusting, friendly attitudes and increases a willingness among members to respond helpfully to one another's needs and requests. A competitive process leads to suspicious, hostile attitudes, increases negative responses to one another's requests, and increases a readiness to exploit each other's needs. A cooperative process enables participants to approach the mutually acknowledged problem in a way that utilizes their talents; it enables them to substitute for each other in their joint work so that duplicate effort is reduced. A competitive process stimulates the view that the solution to a conflict can only be imposed by one side on the other.[10]

On two separate occasions when competition became an issue, Jesus took time to correct his followers. On one occasion, the mother of sons of Zebedee asked Jesus to grant her a favor: she wanted one of her sons to sit at his right hand while the other sat at his left when he came into his kingdom. When the other ten disciples heard her request, they became indignant with the two brothers. Jesus answered them by saying, "Whoever wants to become great among you must be your servant, and whoever wants to be first must be your slave."[11] On another occasion, the disciples found themselves arguing about who among them was the greatest. Again, Jesus told them that "if anyone wants to be first, he must be the very last and a servant of all."[12]

A year ago, I had a conflict with an employee that could have been avoided if I had taken the time to test people's perceptions before I began to advocate my position. This member of the company's professional staff had been given new responsibilities in an area in which she had no direct experience. She perceived herself as being capable while I perceived her as just the opposite: incompetent. What had started out as giving helpful advice soon turned into a heated argument. I could not understand why she could not see the error of her ways; I was the recognized expert, but she persisted in her position. Even though I apologized for letting the discussion escalate, the damage had been done and the relationship was never the same. Technically, I was right. But I paid a heavy price for the satisfaction of letting her know it. If I had once stopped to check my perceptions with hers before proceeding, the entire incident could have been avoided.

Resistance to moving away from competition to cooperation may stem from a loss of power and authority—the pay and glory of certain positions. The toughest obstacle that hinders self-directed teams is management's unwillingness to give up control. This unwillingness to give up control is also a potential source of conflict. The learning community allows for a person to examine one's own mental models in an environment where people support each other as friends. The community building process allows people the opportunity to build relationships that will ward off conflict when it surfaces. Effective methods of conflict resolution are consistent with the values of the learning community because they set the preservation of the relationship as its primary objective.

ENDNOTES

[1] Roger Fisher and William Ury, *Getting to Yes: Negotiating Agreement Without Giving In* (New York: Penguin Books, 1991), 36-37.

[2] James A. Schellengerg, *Conflict Resolution: Theory, Research, and Practice* (Albany: State University of New York, 1996), 23.

[3] Weeks, *The Eight Essential Steps to Conflict Resolution*, 29.

[4] Ibid., 71-234.

[5] Fisher and Ury, *Getting to Yes,* 36-37.

[6] Ibid.,15.

[7] Morton Deutsch, *The Resolution of Conflict: Constructive and Destructive Process* (New Haven: Yale University Press, 1973), 5-7.

[8] Ibid., 26.

[9] Ibid. 29-30.

[10] Matt. 20:20-27 NIV.

[11] Mark 9:33-35 NIV.

[12] W. A. Dimma "Competitive Strategic Planning" *Business Quarterly* 50, 1 (spring 1985): 22.

CHAPTER EIGHT

STRATEGIC PLANNING

In order for the learning community to be effective, its values must permeate every aspect of the organization including strategic planning. Strategic planning is an opportunity for every person to participate in the planning process in order to contribute to the future success of the organization. Strategic planning is primarily concerned with the future—planning today to prepare for tomorrow. William A. Dimma, chief executive officer of Royal Lepage Ltd., a large Canadian financial organization, stated simply, "there are only four ways I know to deal with the future. You can ignore it, predict it, control it or you can respond to it."[1] Strategic planning has to do with either predicting the future or trying to control it. Ignoring the future or simply responding to the future is not strategic planning.

The concept of the learning community offers an alternative process to the traditional top down strategic planning process. A typical management book definition of strategy is "top management's plans to attain outcomes consistent with organization's missions and goals."[2] The traditional top down process is exclusive, whereas the learning community process is inclusive. One of the basic assumptions put forth in this book is best stated by James Surowiecki in his book *The Wisdom of Crowds*. He states, "If you put together a big enough and diverse enough group of people and ask them make decisions affecting matters of general interest, that group's decisions will, over time, be intellectually superior to the isolated individual, no matter how smart or well-informed the individual."[3] If we accept this assumption, then putting together a diverse group of people and asking them to make strategic planning decisions enables decisions to be superior to the isolated individual, no matter how smart or well-informed the individual.

One common perception about strategy is that strategy sets the direction for the organization. The advantage is that strategy provides a map to follow through the future. The disadvantage is that if the organization is too focused on one direction, it may fail to see potential hazards. Doing this would be like setting sail on a fixed heading without paying attention to other boats in the area set on a collision course with your boat.

There are two types of strategies: deliberate and emergent. Deliberate strategy is an intended plan, whereas emergent strategy is a realized pattern. Using the sailing metaphor, the deliberate strategy would be the intentional plan to sail in a specific direction at a predetermined speed. An emergent strategy would consider the pattern of the trip by recognizing changing winds, currents and shallow reefs. The emergent strategies are not necessarily bad, as deliberate strategies are not always good. Effective strategies mix both in ways that reflect the conditions at hand, notably the ability to predict as well as the need to react to unexpected events. Deliberate strategy focuses on control by making sure that managerial intentions are realized. Emergent strategy emphasizes learning by coming to understand through the taking action what those intentions should be in the first place.[4]

Mintzberg identifies these two schools of strategic planning as the planning school and the learning school. The planning school relies on a deliberate method of strategic planning. The learning school relies more on emergent strategy. The basic premises of the planning school are as follows:

1. Strategy formation should be controlled and conscious as well as formalized.
2. Responsibility for the overall process rests with the chief executive in principle; responsibility for its execution rests with the staff planners.
3. Strategies come out of planning process fully developed.
4. Strategies are implemented through detailed attention to objectives, budgets, programs, and operating plans of various kinds.[5]

Mitzenburg's Five Fallacies of the Planning School

Mitzenburg, in his book *The Rise and Fall of Strategic Planning*, identifies five fallacies of deliberate strategic planning. The first is the fallacy of predetermination: the idea that the future is foreseeable. In reality, forecasting is notoriously inaccurate. If the world could hold still, or at least continue to change exactly as it did in the past, then forecasting would work fine. Forecasting in the 1960s were good times for planners not because their techniques were any better than today, but because the trends at that time were more stable. Forecasting as control infers that predicting can enact its environment. Enactment planning requires some kind of closed system, one that doesn't change. Unfortunately, perfectly closed systems just do not exist.

Scenario building, another forecasting tool, is predicated on the assumption that if the future cannot be predicted, then speculating upon a variety of them might just hit upon the right one. Peter Schwartz, in his book *The Art of the Long View*, reports the success Royal Dutch/Shell Group had in the 1980s when they developed scenarios speculating that Gorbachev would come to power and that the Soviet Union would enter the world oil market. That scenario came to fruition, resulting in a collapse in oil prices. The Royal Dutch/Shell Group had positioned itself to take advantage of this drop which allowed them to buy oil reserves at half the price they would have had to pay six months prior.[6] Scenarios are predicated on the ability to identify the driving forces that influence the future. But detached planners are less likely to be in touch with these leading indicators. There is also the problem of deciding how many scenarios to build or what to do once these have been built. Michael Porter, author of *Competitive Advantage*, suggested five possibilities: (1) bet on the most probable one, (2) bet on the best one for the firm, (3) hedge so as to get satisfactory results no matter which one occurs, (4) preserve flexibility, or (5) go out and exert influence to make the most desirable scenario a reality.[7] However, changing the managerial worldview often proves to be a much more demanding task. Even after a scenario is built, the process can fail because of the inability to influence the necessary powers that be, namely to convince management to agree with the prediction and to act accordingly. This is one of the major obstacles Schwartz had to overcome before the Royal Dutch/Shell

Group could make the necessary changes to position itself in the event that that scenario became a reality.

The second fallacy is the idea that planners can effectively function in isolation, separated from the day to day operations. This idea includes the detachment of planners from strategy making. In reality, each manager is the nerve center of his or her own unit; and by having personal access to each subordinate, the manager is provided with the broadest information base about that unit. Information relevant to the manager's unit is not available to planners who are detached from strategy making. For example, the President of the United States should be able to know more about the government as a whole than any other individual by virtue of his ability to access every department. The assessment of strengths and weaknesses made by detached planners may be unreliable because they are often bound up with the aspirations, biases, and hopes of those planners. More seriously, these distortions seem to be greatest at the senior managerial levels where strategies are supposed to be formulated. In order to be effective, those who implement strategy must become the formulators of it. Strengths and weaknesses are situational: internal capability can be assessed only with respect to the external context (i.e., markets, political forces, competitors, etc.).

The third fallacy separates thinking from acting. This is the idea that thinking is the responsibility of top management, while acting out plans developed by higher ups is the responsibility of the front line people. To think strategically, managers must be active, involved, connected, committed, alert, and stimulated. A decision is a commitment to future action. Likewise, planning is about the future, not the present. The survival of every organization depends on its actions in the moving present. Thinking must certainly precede action; it must also follow action close behind or else run the risk of impeding it.

The fourth fallacy is the belief that formalization is needed. Formalization is a step-by-step process of gathering data and developing specific operations to use the data to plan for the future. Yet formal planning discourages creativity. People, not rigid systems, produce innovation. If anything has been learned about creativity, it is that it cannot happen in isolation, on schedule, or on demand. A particular weakness of the analytic mind is its tendency toward premature closure: problems are structured early and the alternatives delineated prematurely so that attention can be concentrated on assessing them. Planning and strategy are different: strategy formation establishes categories and planning takes over to enact them.

The fifth fallacy is the false belief that analysis equals synthesis. Analysis is *not* synthesis; strategic planning is not strategy formation. Analysis by nature dissects while synthesis brings together to form something new. The two terms are opposites. No amount of elaboration will ever enable formal procedures to forecast discontinuities, to inform managers who are detached from their operations, or to create novel strategies. Ultimately, the term strategic planning has proven to be an oxymoron. Several decades of experience with strategic planning has demonstrated the need to loosen up the process of strategy formation rather than trying to seal it off through arbitrary formalization.[8]

Research into the effectiveness of strategic planning also casts questions on some of the methodology used by organizations. In 1991, B. K. Boyd published a long and detailed meta-analytic review in the *Journal of Management Studies*. In the twenty-nine empirical studies which sampled 2,496 organizations, he found "the overall effect of planning on performance…very weak."[9] Research by the U.S. Planning Forum found that only 25 percent of companies considered their planning to be effective.[10] Soon after he arrived on the scene as chairman and chief executive officer in the early 1980s, Jack Welch dismantled General Electric's strategic planning system. Welch reduced the corporate planning group from fifty-seven to thirty-three, and scores of planners were eliminated in the company's operating sectors, groups and divisions.[11]

Also, several existing research studies have suggested that environmental volatility and unpredictability might effect a firm's strategic planning in the following ways: (a) forcing a redistribution of authority in strategic planning from the corporate center to a more decentralized business group, (b) shortening the planning horizon as a result of greater uncertainty about the future, and (c) reducing the formality of the planning process.[12]

To illustrate, in 1999, I was instrumental in taking my church through the strategic planning process very much in line with the planning school model. The strategy formation was controlled, conscious, and formalized; and the strategic planning team was selected from a cross section of the church. The team conducted a SWOT analysis assessing the churches strengths, weaknesses, opportunities and threats, and then met to formulate the church's vision statement, values, goals and objectives. Although the senior pastor was very involved in the process, the execution rested with me, the staff planner. The church staff was then given the responsibility to develop strategies based on the goals and objectives developed by the strategic planning team. While these subsequent strategies needed to meet the specific objectives set by the formation team, the church staff was never asked if these objectives were achievable or realistic. Once the team had completed their strategy work, they disbanded. There was no provision for the strategic planning team to regroup to review the effectiveness of the strategies.

Ultimately, although the senior pastor effectively communicated the vision statement to the congregation, the strategic plan received little attention after it was distributed to the congregation. The church's deliberate strategy attempted to implement small groups into the church as a whole; but when emergent strategies surfaced, there was no process in place to learn from the initial strategies. Instead, the leadership of the church changed strategy without modifying the strategic plan. Leadership operated as if the strategic plan was cast in stone until the five-year period had expired and a new strategic planning process could be initiated. Any change to the plan would have been construed as an admission of failure instead of an opportunity to learn. The existing plan was later modified in an attempt to render it useful, but it never served the purpose for which it was intended. This experience demonstrated that holding to a rigid mental model that believes strategic plans cannot be changed is much like establishing a fixed course without having the ability to change regardless of wind direction, weather, or other boats in the area. As in sailing, the measure of a successful trip is not whether the exact planned course was followed, but that everyone arrived at the intended destination without risk to the safety of the crew and or vessel.

The only relevant learning in a company is the learning done by those people who have the power to act. Because of this, the real purpose of effective planning is not to make plans, but to change the mental models held by decision makers. In this role as facilitator, catalyst, and accelerator of the corporate planning process, planners are apt to fall into several traps. One is that they sometimes start with a mental model that is unrecognizable to their audience. Another is that they take too many steps at once. The third and most serious trap is that they too often communicate their information by teaching. This is a natural trap to fall into because it is how most people have been conditioned throughout their lives. But teaching, as John Holt points out, is actually one of the least efficient ways to convey knowledge. At best, 40 percent of what is taught is received; in most situations, it is only about 25 percent. Teaching has another disadvantage as well, especially in a business setting: teachers must be given authority by their students based on the teacher's presumed superior understanding. When you cannot be granted authority, you can no longer teach. The best learning takes place in teams that accept that the whole is larger than the sum of the parts, that there is a good that transcends the individual. Institutional learning begins with the calibration of existing mental models.[13]

There are numerous benefits to adopting a strategic planning process that is inclusive in nature and encourages everyone in the organization to participate. People are much more motivated when they participate in the development of their own plans instead of the plans of others. According to B. M. Bass, in an article published in the *Journal of Applied Behavioral Science* in 1970, people were less productive and less satisfied when they operated other people's plans instead of their own. Bass suggested a number of reasons for this. First, productivity and satisfaction reduce when planning for others because the sense of accomplishment is less when executing someone else's plan. Second, there are fewer tendencies to try to confirm the validity of another's plan by executing it successfully because there is less confidence that it can be done. Third, there is less commitment to see that the plan works well. Fourth, there is less flexibility and less room for modification and initiative to make improvements in an assigned plan, and there is less understanding of an assigned plan. Fifth, human resources are not well utilized because there are more communication problems that have consequent errors and more distortions in following instructions. Finally, competitive feelings are aroused between planners and doers to such an extent that it appears that the former win and the latter lose.[14]

Incorporating people into the planning and learning process improves satisfaction and productivity. People become part of the learning process as information flows through the entire organization, making management teams and direct-line people a part of institutional learning. Institutional learning is the process whereby management teams change their shared mental models of their company, their markets, and their competitors. For this reason, management thinks of planning as learning and of corporate planning as institutional learning. The premises of the learning school are consistent with the values of the learning community and empower members of the organization to participate and learn as an institution. The premises of the learning school are as follows:

1. The complex and unpredictable nature of the organization's environment, often coupled with the diffusion of knowledge bases needed for strategy, precludes deliberate control. Strategy making must above all become a process of learning over time. At its limit, formulation and implementation become indistinguishable.
2. While the leader must also learn and may sometimes be the main learner, more commonly, it is the group that learns. There are many potential strategies in most organizations.
3. This learning proceeds in an emergent fashion through behavior that stimulates thinking retrospectively.
4. The role of leadership thus becomes not to preconceive deliberate strategies, but to manage the process of strategic learning whereby novel strategies can emerge.
5. Accordingly, strategies appear first as patterns out of the past, and only later, perhaps, as plans for the future. Ultimately, they are perspectives to guide overall behavior.[15]

Strategy Formation and the Learning Community

Mitzenburg's grassroots model of strategy formation is consistent with the values of a learning community. His model is as follows:

1. Strategies grow initially like weeds in a garden; they are not cultivated like tomatoes in a hothouse. It is more important to let patterns emerge than to force an artificial consistency.
2. These strategies can take root in all kinds of places, virtually anywhere people have the capacity to learn and the resources to support that capacity.

3. Such strategies become organizational when they become collective; that is, when the patterns proliferate to pervade the behavior of the organization at large.
4. The processes of proliferation may be conscious, but need not be; likewise, they may be managed, but need not be.
5. New strategies, which may be emerging continuously, tend to pervade the organization during periods of change, which punctuate periods of more integrated continuity.
6. To management, this process exists not to preconceive strategies, but to recognize their emergence and to intervene when appropriate.[16]

Strategic planning is primarily concerned with predicting or controlling the future. It is the responsibility of everyone in the organization to share this common concern. The future is no longer static but dynamic. It requires that everyone who has the capacity to learn to be involved in the formulation and implementation of strategy. The learning community becomes an integral part of the learning process to review strategy and modify plans to address a constantly changing environment.

Igor Ansoff, considered by many in the industry as the "godfather of corporate strategy," saw strategic planning as a complex sequence of decisions. As such, he defined an important concept known as the gap analysis, the gap being the difference between the current position of an organization and its strategic objectives. In the next chapter, this gap between the current reality of the organization and the ideal of a learning organization will be measured. Performance management is the process of evaluating progress toward closing the gap.

ENDNOTES

1 P. Wright, C. Pringle, and M. Droll, *Strategic Management Text and Cases* (Needham Heights: Allyn and Bacon, 1992), 101.

2 James Surowiecki, *The Wisdom of Crowds: Why the Many are Smarter than the Few and How Collective Wisdom Shapes Business, Economics, Societies and Nations* (New York: Doubleday, 2004), xvii

3 Henry Mintzberg *Strategy Safari: A Guided Tour Through the Wilds of Strategic Management* (New York: The Free Press, 1998), 10-15.

4 Ibid, 58.

5 Peter Schwartz, *The Art of the Long View: Planning for the Future in an Uncertain World* (New York: Doubleday, 1991), 54-55.

6 Michael Porter, *Competitive Advantage*: *Creating and Sustaining Superior Performance* (New York: Free Press, 1985), 82.

7 Henry Mintzberg *The Rise and Fall of Strategic Planning*: Reconceiving Roles for Planning, Plans, Planners (New York: Macmillan, 1994), 221-321.

8 B. K. Boyd "Strategic Planning and Financial Performance: A Meta-Analytical Review." *Journal of Management Studies* XXXVIII (July 1991), 353.

9 Nick Philipson, ed., *Business: The Ultimate Resource* (Cambridge: *Perseus*, 2002), 949.

10 Mintzberg, *The Rise and Fall of Strategic Planning*, 103.

11 Roger M. Grant, "Strategic Planning in a Turbulent Environment: Evidence from the Oil Majors" *Strategic Management Journal* 24, no. 6, (2003), 491.

12 Arie De Geus "Planning as Learning" *Harvard Business Review* 66, no. 2 (March-April 1988), 70-75.

13 B. M. Bass "When Planning for Others" *Journal of Applied Behavioral Science* VI, no. 2, (April/May/June 1970): 151-171.

14 Mintzberg, *Strategy Safari*, 208.

15 Ibid, 196-198.

16 Douglas McGregor, "An Uneasy Look at Performance Appraisal" *Harvard Business Review* 46, no. 6 (September/October 1972): 66.

CHAPTER NINE

PERFORMANCE MANAGEMENT

Anyone who has traveled any distance by car with children in the back seat are familiar with the phrase, Are we there yet? In this transitional process of becoming a learning organization, everyone in the organization wants to know the same thing. The strategic planning process lays out the road map, and the performance management process provides the mile markers that tell how close the destination is.

In the past, the only two measurement tools available to me were financial statements and performance appraisals. Company success was measured based on financial statements, and employee performance was measured using an annual performance appraisal. If the company was making money and everyone was doing their job, I was content with the organization's performance. However, the purpose of the learning community is to transform the organization into a learning organization. Transformation measurements do not show up on financial statements or on standard performance evaluations.

My use of performance appraisals has covered the full gamut of various formats: from rating scales, to narratives, to 360-degree feedback systems. These were intended to give people feedback to motivate them to improve their skills. In reality, they created anxiety and left people demoralized. In addition they were time consuming and produced very few positive results.

Performance Management and the Learning Community

The learning community incorporates a process where people determine how they are going to contribute to the success of the organization's strategies and evaluate their own performance. First, it empowers people to take responsibility and ownership in the process. The underlying assumptions of traditional performance appraisals differ from the assumptions established by a learning community. The traditional performance appraisal assumes that commitment can be forced. In a learning community commitment can best be nurtured through a supportive network, environment, encouragement, a compelling vision, education, and most of all choices. Second, the traditional performance appraisal assumes the organization and the supervisor are responsible for employee feedback, development, and performance. In the learning community, its members are responsible for their own feedback, performance, and development, with support from the organization. Third, the traditional performance appraisal process assumes that ratings motivate by letting people know where they stand. But in the learning community, ratings undermine commitment and demoralize. Fourth, the traditional performance appraisal process assumes that inspecting individuals leads to improvement, and improving individual performance improves organizational performance. In contrast, the learning community proposes that the improving of systems and processes improves the performance of the organization. Improvement results from identifying and studying the cause of the problem, developing a plan, learning, and acting on the information learned. The challenge of the learning community is to design a performance management system that facilitates commitment and accountability instead of destroying them.

Douglas McGregor, the author of the best-seller *The Human Side of Enterprise*, identified some of the same problems present today that existed fifty-years ago. He states, "Managers admit to the necessity but balk at the process. For several good reasons: They dislike criticizing, lack of skill and a mistrust of the validity of the appraisal instrument. The conventional approach is a violation of the integrity of the personality. It is judging the personal worth of a fellow man. It forces us to make judgments and communicate them to those we have judged. Trying to help is inconsistent with judgments. It reflects an unwillingness to treat human beings like physical objects."[1]

Dr. W. Edwards Deming, one of the founders of Total Quality Management, noted, "The annual review nourishes short-term performance, annihilates long-term planning, builds fear, demolishes teamwork, nourishes rivalry and politics. . . . It leaves people bitter, crushed, bruised, battered, desolate, despondent, dejected, feeling inferior, some even depressed, unfit for work for weeks after receipt of rating, unable to comprehend why they are inferior. It is unfair, as it ascribes to the people in a group differences that may be caused totally by the system that they work in."[2]

McGregor offers a new approach that shifts the responsibility of the appraisal process from the supervisor to the subordinate. In this approach, the subordinate spends time thinking about his or her job; and after a careful assessment of personal strengths and weaknesses, formulates specific plans to accomplish short-term goals. The supervisor's role is to help the person establish goals and appraise his or her own performance instead of the supervisor. This approach fits well with the values of the learning community. The supervisor becomes a coach who helps the person define personal areas of responsibility and then establish goals that contribute to the strategic goals of the organization. At the conclusion of a six month period, the subordinate makes his or her own appraisal of what has been accomplished. The interview step is an examination of the self-appraisal and culminates in a resetting of targets for the next six months.[3] This approach to performance appraisal differs from the standard appraisal because it shifts the emphasis from appraisal to analysis. The subordinate is no longer being examined by the superior, rather he is examining himself. This approach preserves the values of the learning community while achieving the goals of the organization.

In order to measure the performance of the organization, a process needs to provide accurate feedback as the organization begins to change the way it conducts its internal business. The process of evaluating organization performance requires more than a review of the financial statements at the end of the month. The Balanced Scorecard, developed by Robert Kaplan and David Norton, provides a framework to translate a strategy into operational terms. It allows the learning community to identify cause and effect relationships that help close the gap between where the organization is today and where it wants to be in the future. This scorecard is organized around four distinct perspectives: financial, customer, internal business process, and learning and growth. Each organization has its own way of addressing financial, customer, and internal business processes, depending on its industry. However, every organization must answer how to achieve their vision and how to sustain the ability to change and improve. This discussion focuses on three principal categories for learning and growth perspectives: employee capabilities, information systems capabilities and motivation, and empowerment and alignment.[4]

The Balanced Scorecard integrates with the performance evaluation process by using of a number of various assessments. These assessments may measure a number of areas such as leadership, employee satisfaction, and any other area the organization deems important. For purposes of this explanation, the organization will be assessed to determine if the current practices are consistent with those of a learning organization. Virginia Marsick and Karen Watkins developed an assessment instrument that measures the seven dimensions of a learning organization that can be used in conjunction with the Balanced Scorecard. The Dimensions of the Learning Organization Questionnaire (DLOQ), consists of fifty-five statements about organization practices. Respondents indicate the degree to which they perceive these practices occurring, using a six-point scale ranging from almost always to almost never. The items are then organized by three levels—individual, team, and organization—in terms of the seven dimensions of the learning organization.[5]

If the DLOQ assessment determines there is a gap between what a learning organization practices and how the present organization functions, then closing that gap becomes a strategic objective. For example, assume that an assessment revealed a gap in employee perception of being rewarded for learning. Impacting employee awareness of learning rewards should then become the strategic objective. A strategy is a set of hypotheses about cause and effect. It becomes the responsibility of the learning community to formulate a cause-and-effect statement regarding employee perception of learning rewards. An example of this cause-and-effect statement could be: If the company develops a company policy reimbursing employees who complete college courses, then employees will perceive the company as an organization that rewards learning. Lead indicators drive performance: they cause change. In this example, the lead indicator, or performance driver, is the new policy offering tuition assistance. Lag indicators measure the following effect of the performance driver. In this case, a higher score on the DLOQ would be the lag indicator. The table below shows how these three components would appear on a balanced scorecard.[6]

Table 1. Balanced Scorecard Example

STRATEGIC OBJECTIVES	STRATEGIC MEASUREMENTS	
Learning and Growth	Lag Indicators	Lead Indicators
Reward staff for learning	*DLOQ assessment outcomes*	*Implement new tuition assistance program*

The intent of the performance appraisal process integrates each person's job plan with the Balanced Scorecard. Douglas Sherwin, in his article "The Job of Job Evaluation," proposes the concept of a job plan that consists of three parts: a job description, a performance description, and a performance evaluation. The job description states the intent, the performance description identifies what actually happened, and the performance evaluation determines how much the performance is worth to the organization.[7] It is in the job description where each person identifies their intent to contribute to the strategic objective within the Balanced Scorecard. In the above example, the employee's job plan would contain the following three parts:

1. *Job Description.* The employee will seek out new learning opportunities and receive additional compensation for this effort.
2. *Job Performance.* The employee enrolled in a college course and was reimbursed for tuition.
3. *Job Evaluation.* The employee now has new knowledge that warrants a pay raise.

Integrating the strategic objectives from the Balanced Scorecard into each person's job plan ensures that every person in the organization is focused on the same goals and objectives. It is also important for the coach to ensure that the employee has followed up with action on his or her intent stated in the job description. This is helpful when the learning community reviews the effectiveness of a strategy to determine if employees actually attempted to implement it.

The last step in the process is a periodic review of the strategies in the strategic plan. Twice a year, the learning community determines if the performance drivers have their intended impact. This is an opportunity for the organization to learn from its previous initiatives. The strategic plan becomes a living document that adapts to changes in the internal and external environment. Each person in the learning organization is responsible for being aware of what performance drivers impact the organization. The ability to learn and adapt is the basic ingredient that constitutes a learning organization.

Conclusion

When a learning organization is finally established, the people in the organization may no longer be perceived as members of the crew but as partners in an adventure. You may see them as being capable of greater skills and responsibility. They may even have the ability to lead themselves. They may develop the ability to resolve conflicts without harm to their relationships. They may be able to see the urgency for change and do so willingly. They may be able to set goals for the organization and welcome being held accountable for those goals. They may regard each other as friends and not as adversaries. They may develop an insatiable appetite for learning that has the potential to transform their lives. They may replace arrogance with a sense of humility, knowing that no one has all the answers.

ENDNOTES

1. W. Edwards Deming, *Out of the Crisis* (Cambridge: Massachusetts Institute of Technology, 1986), 102.
2. McGregor, "An Uneasy Look at Performance Appraisal," 67.
3. Robert S. Kaplan and David P. Norton, *The Balanced Scorecard: Translating Strategy Into Action* (Boston: Harvard Business School Press, 1996), 127.
4. Virginia Marsick and Karen Watkins, "Dimensions of the Learning Organization Questionnaire" [instructions online]; available from http://partnersforlearning.com/instructions.html; Internet.
5. Kaplan and Norton, *The Balanced Scorecard*, 237.
6. Douglas S. Sherwin, "The Job of Job Evaluation" *Harvard Business Review* 35, no. 3, (May/June, 1957): 63.

SELECTED BIBLIOGRAPHY

Argyris, C. and D. A. Schon. *Organizational Learning II: Theory, Method and Practice*. New York: Addison-Wesley 1996.

Barker, J. A. *Paradigms: The Business of Discovering the Future*. New York: HarperCollins, 1992.

Barker, K. ed. *New International Version Study Bible*. Grand Rapids: Zondervan 1995.

Bass, B. *Bass & Stogdill's Handbook of Leadership: Theory, Research & Managerial Applications,* 3rd ed. New York: Free Press, 1990.

Bass, B. "When Planning for Others," *Journal of Applied Behavioral Science* VII, no. 2 (April/May/June 1970): 151-171.

Belasco, J. "The leader as partner-coach and people developer." In *Partnering: The New Face of Leadership*, eds. S. Larraine, M. Goldsmith and J. Belasco. New York: AMACOM Books, 2003.

Blake, R. R. and A. A. McCanse. *Leadership Dilemmas—Grid Solutions*. Houston: Gulf Publishing, 1991.

Blake, R. R. and J. S. Mouton. "Grid Principles Versus Situationalism: A Final Note," *Group and Organizational Studies* (June 1982): 7, No. 2 211-215.

___. The *Managerial Grid III: The Key to Leadership Excellence*. Houston: Excellence Gulf, 1985.

Blanchard, S. and M. Homan. *Leverage Your Best, Ditch the Rest*. New York: HarperCollins, 2004.

Blanchard, K. "Leadership Partnering for Performance Using Situational Leadership." In *Partnering: The New Face of Leadership*, eds. S. Larraine, M. Goldsmith and J. Belasco. New York: AMACOM Books, 2003.

Block, P. *The Answer to How is Yes: Acting on What Matters.* San Francisco: Berrett- Koehler, 2002.

Borden, P. *Hit the Bullseye: How Denominations Can Aim the Congregation at the Mission Field.* Nashville: Abingdon Press, 2003.

Boyd, B. K. "Strategic planning and financial performance: a meta-analytical review," *Journal of Management Studies* XXXVIII (July1991): 353-375.

Collins, J.C. and J. I. Porras. *Built to Last: Successful Habits of Visionary Companies.* New York: HarperCollins, 1997.

Daft, R.L. *Mangement,* 3rd ed. New York: Dryden Press, 1994.

"Definitions of Leadership: Ten Worth Remembering." 2005. Article online. Available from http://www.legacee.com/Info/Leadership/Definitions.html; Internet.

De Geus, A. "Planning as Learning," *Harvard Business Review* 66, no. 2 (March-April 1998): 70-75.

Deming, W. E. *Out of the Crisis.* Cambridge: Massachusetts Institute of Technology Press, 1986.

Dent, S. M. *Partnering Intelligence: Creating Value for Your Business by Building Strong Alliances.* Palo Alto: Davis-Black, 1999.

Deutsch, M. *The Resolution of Conflict: Constructive and Destructive Process.* New Haven: Yale University Press, 1973.

Dimma, W. A. "Competitive Strategic Planning," *Business Quarterly* 50, no. 1 (spring 1985): 22.

Fisher, K. *Leading Self-Directed Work Teams: A Guide to Developing New Leadership Skills.* New York: McGraw-Hill, 1993.

Fisher, R. and W. Ury. *Getting to Yes: Negotiating Agreement Without Giving In.* New York: Penguin Books, 1991.

Flaherty, J. *Coaching: Evoking Excellence in Others.* Woburn: Butterworth-Heineman, 1999.

Gallwey, T. *The Inner Game of Tennis.* New York: Random House, 1986.

Garvin, D. A. "Building Learning Organizations," *Harvard Business Review* 71, no. 4 (July-August 1993): 19-29.

Gibbs, J. *Tribes: A New Way of Learning and Being Together.* Windsor: Center Source Systems, 2001.

___. "About Tribes" (2005) [article online]; available from http://www. tribes.com/ article_research.htm; Internet.

Goleman, D. *Emotional Intelligence: Why It Can Matter More Than I.Q.* New York: Bantam Books, 1994.

Graen, G., M. A. Novak, and P. Sommerkamp. "The effects of leader-member exchange and job design on productivity and satisfaction: Testing a dual attachment model." *Organizational Behavior and Human Performance* 30 (1982): 109-131.

Grant, R. M. "Strategic Planning in a Turbulent Environment: Evidence from the Oil Majors. *Strategic Management Journal* 24, no. 6 (2003): 491.

Greenleaf, R. *Servant As Leader,* 1970. Quoted in "What is Servant-Leadership." Article online; Available from http://www.greenleaf. org/leadership/servant-leadership/What-is-Servant-Leadership. html; Internet.

Hackman, M. Z. and C. E. Johnston. *Leadership: A Communication Perspective.* Prospect Heights: Waveland Press, 1996.

Hersey, P., K. H. Blanchard, and D. E. Johnson. *Management of Organizational Behavior: Utilizing Human Resources,* 7th ed. Upper Saddle River: Prentice-Hall, 1996.

Howe, R. L. *The Miracle of Dialogue.* New York: Seabury Press, 1963.

Janis, I. *Groupthink*, 2nd ed. Boston: Houghton Mifflin, 1982. Quoted in Jean Lipman- Blumen and Harold J. Leavitt, *Hot Groups: Seeding Them, Feeding Them, & Using Them to Ignite Your Organization.* New York: Oxford University Press, 1996.

Jennings, E.E. "The Anatomy of Leadership," *Management of Personnel Quarterly* 1, no. 1 (autumn1961): 2-10.

Kanter, R. M. *Commitment and Community: Communities and Utopias in Sociological Perspective.* Cambridge: Harvard University Press, 1972.

Kaplan, R. S. and D. P. Norton. *The Balanced Scorecard: Translating Strategy Into Action*. Boston: Harvard Business School Press, 1996.

___. "Use the Balanced Scorecard to Partner with Strategic Constituents." In *Partnering: The New Face of Leadership*, eds. S. Larraine, M. Goldsmith and J. Belasco. New York: AMACOM Books, 2003.

Kotter, J. P. *Leading Change*. Boston: Harvard Business School Press, 1996.

___. "Kill Complacency," *Fortune* 13, no. 3 (August 1996): 168. "Leading by Vision and Strategy" *Executive Excellence* 14, no. 10 (October 1997): 15.

Kouzes, J. M. and B. Z. Posner. "Leaders Must Build Cultures of Collaboration." In *Partnering: The New Face of Leadership*, eds. S. Larraine, M. Goldsmith and J. Belasco. New York: AMACOM Books, 2003.

Levine, J. H. and N. Shapiro. *Creating Learning Communities: A Practical Guide to Winning Support, Organizing for Change, and Implementing Programs*. San Francisco: John Willey & Sons, 1999.

Likert, R. *New Patterns of Management*. New York: McGraw-Hill, 1961.

Lipman-Blumen, J. and H. J. Leavitt. *Hot Groups: Seeding Them, Feeding Them, & Using Them to Ignite Your Organization*. New York: Oxford University Press, 1996.

Logan, Robert E. and Sherilyn Carlton. "Coaching 101." Article online. Available from http://coachnet.org/admin/files/upload/coachmodel.pdf. Internet.

Manz, C. C. and H. P. Sims Jr. *The New SuperLeadership: Leading Others to Lead Themselves*. San Francisco: Berrett-Koehler, 2001.

Marsick, V. and K. Watkins. *In Action: Creating the Learning Organization*. Alexandria: American Society for Training Development, 1996.

___. *Dimensions of the Learning Organization Questionnaire*. Warwick: Partners for the Learning Organization, 1997. Questionnaire online. Available from http://www.partnersforlearning.com /instructions. html. Internet.

Maxwell, J. *21 Irrefutable Laws of Leadership*. Nashville: Thomas Nelson, 2002. Quoted in "What is Leadership." (2005). Article online.

Available from http://www.teal.org.uk/Leadership/ definition.htm; Internet.

Malphurs, A. *Values-Driven Leadership: Discovering and Developing Your Core Values for Ministry.* Grand Rapids: Baker Books, 1996.

McGregor, D. *The Human Side of Enterprise.* New York: McGraw-Hill, 1960.. "An Uneasy Look at Performance Appraisal," *Harvard Business \ Review* 46, no. 6 (September-October 1972): 66.

Merriam-Webster's Collegiate Dictionary, 11th ed. Springfield: Merriam-Webster, 2004.

Mintzberg, H. *Mintzberg on Management: Inside Our Strange World of Organizations.* New York: Free Press, 1989.

___. *The Rise and Fall of Strategic Planning: Reconceiving Roles for Planning, Plans, Planners.* New York: Macmillan, 1994.

Mintzberg, H., B. Ahlstrand and A. J. Lampel. *Strategy Safari: A Guided Tour Through the Wilds of Strategic Management.* New York: Free Press, 1998.

Marston, W. M. *The Emotions of Normal People.* Minneapolis: Persona Press, 1979.

Moxley, R. S. and J. R. Alexander "Leadership-as-Partnership." In *Partnering: The New Face of Leadership*, eds. S. Larraine, M. Goldsmith and J. Belasco. New York: AMACOM Books, 2003.

Nelson, B. "Rub Somebody the Right Way." In *Partnering: The New Face of Leadership*, eds. S. Larraine, M. Goldsmith and J. Belasco. New York: AMACOM Books, 2003.

Nelson, D. R. and D. P. Witmer. "Developing a Learning Community Approach to Business Education." *Teaching Business Ethics* 5, no. 3 (August 2001): 267-281

O'Brien, M. "Personal Mastery: The New Executive Curriculum" *Training* 33, no. 7 (July 1996): 82.

Peck, M. S. *The Different Drum: Community Making and Peace.* New York: Simon & Schuster, 1987.

Peters, T.J. and R. Waterman. *In Search of Excellence: Lessons from America's Best-Run Companies.* New York: Harper-Collins, 1998.

Philipson, N. ed. *Business: The Ultimate Resource.* Cambridge: *Perseus Publishing*, 2002.

Pinchot, E. and G. Pinchot. "Leading Organizations into Partnership." In *Partnering: The New Face of Leadership*, eds. S. Larraine, M. Goldsmith and J. Belasco. New York: AMACOM Books, 2003.

Porter, M. *Competitive Advantage*: Creating and Sustaining Superior Performance. New York: Free Press, 1985.

Quinn, R. E. *Deep Change: Discovering the Leader Within*. San Francisco: Jossey-Bass, 2003.

Robbins, H. A. and M. Finley. *The New Why Teams Don't Work: What Goes Wrong and How to Make it Right*. San Francisco: Berrett-Joehler, 2000.

Rokeach, M. *Understanding Human Values: Individual and Societal*. New York: Macmillan, 1979.

Romig, D. *Side by Side Leadership: Achieving Outstanding Results Together*. Marietta: Bard Press, 2001.

Rosenblum, J. and C. Oates. "The Learning Leader as Partner." In *Partnering: The New Face of Leadership*, eds. S. Larraine, M. Goldsmith and J. Belasco. New York: AMACOM Books, 2003.

Ryan, S. "Emergence of Learning Communities." In *Community Building: Renewing Spirit & Learning in Business*, ed. G. Kaximierz. San Francisco: New Leaders Press, 1995.

Schellengerg, J. A. *Conflict Resolution: Theory, Research, and Practice*. Albany: State University of New York Press, 1996.

Schwartz, P. *The Art of the Long View: Planning for the Future in an Uncertain World*. New York: Doubleday, 1991.

Senge, P. M. "Communities of Commitment: the Heart of Learning Organizations," *Organizational Dynamics* 22, no. 2 (autumn 1993): 5-23.

_____. "Creating Change." *Executive Excellence* 17, no. 10 (October2000): 4-5.

_____. "Learning Leaders." *Executive Excellence* 16, no. 11 (November 1999): 12-13.

_____. "Mental Models." *Planning Review* 20, no. 2 (March-April 1992): 4-12.

_____. *The Fifth Discipline: The Art and Practice of the Learning Organization*. New York: Doubleday Dell, 1990.

___. "The Learning Organization Made Plain." Interview by Patricia A. Galagan, \ *Training & Development* 45, no. 37 (October 1991): 8.

Shaffer, C. and K. Anundsen. *Creating Community Anywhere: Finding Support and Connection in a Fragmented World*. Berkley: Penquin Group, 1993.

Sherwin, D.S. "The Job of Job Evaluation" *Harvard Business Review* 35, no. 3, (May/June 1957): 63.

Smith, M. K. "Peter Senge and The Learning Organization" (2005). Article online. Available from http://infed.org/thinkers/senge.htm; Internet.

Surowiecki, J. *The Wisdom of Crowds: Why the Many are Smarter than the Few and How Collective Wisdom Shapes Business, Economics, Societies and Nations*. New York: Doubleday, 2004.

Ting, S. and W. Hart. "Formal Coaching." In *The Center for Creative Leadership Handbook of Leadership Development*, 2nd ed., eds. C. D. McCauley and E. V. Velsor. San Francisco: John Wiley & Sons, 2004.

Weeks, D. *The Eight Essential Steps to Conflict Resolution: Preserving Relationships at Work, at Home, and in the Community*. New York: G. P. Putnam's Sons, 1992.

Wenger, E. *Communities of Practice: Learning, Meaning, and Identity*. New York: Cambridge University Press, 1998.

"What is Leadership" (2005) [article online]; available from http:// www.teal.org.uk/ Leadership/definition.htm; Internet.

Wright, P., C. Pringle and M. Droll. *Strategic Management Text and Cases*. Needham Heights: Allyn and Bacon, 1992.

Zell, D. "Organizational Change as a Process of Death, Dying and Rebirth," *Journal of Applied Behavioral Science* 39, no. 1 (March 2003): 73-96.

www.ingramcontent.com/pod-product-compliance
Lightning Source LLC
Chambersburg PA
CBHW030008190526
45157CB00014B/1339